Russian/Soviet Submarine Launched Ballistic Missiles

Nuclear Deterrence/Counter Force Strike

HUGH HARKINS

Copyright © 2018 Hugh Harkins

All rights reserved.

ISBN: 1903630681
ISBN-13: 978-1903630686

Russian/Soviet Submarine Launched Ballistic Missiles
Nuclear Deterrence/Counter Force Strike

© Hugh Harkins 2018

Centurion Publishing
United Kingdom

ISBN 10: 1903630681
ISBN 13: 978-1903630686

This volume first published in 2018

The Author is identified as the copyright holder of this work under sections 77 and 78 of the Copyright Designs and Patents Act 1988

Cover design © Createspace Independent Publishing Platform & Centurion Publishing

Page layout, concept and design © Centurion Publishing

All rights reserved. No part of this publication may be reproduced, stored in a retrieval system, transmitted in any form, or by any means, electronic, mechanical or photocopied, recorded or otherwise, without the written permission of the publisher

The publisher and author would like to thank all organisations and services for their assistance and contributions in the preparation of this volume:
JSC Company 'Academician' V. P. Makeyev State Rocket Centre; S. P. Korolev Rocket and Space Corporation, Energia; JSC CB-Arsenal (KB Arsenal) Design Bureau (FSUE); Krasnoyarsk Machine-Building Plant (Factory) (JSC KRASMASH); CDB-Rubin (Central Design Bureau for Marine Engineering Rubin); JSC Production Association 'Northern Machine-Building Enterprise (PA Sevmash); NIPTB Onega (Research and Development Technological Bureau 'Onega'); United Shipbuilding Corporation; Moscow Institute of Thermal Technology; TASS; United States Department of Defence; Central Intelligence Agency and the Ministry of Defense of the Russian Federation

CONTENTS

	INTRODUCTION	i
1	A New Concept in Strategic Strike	1
2	First Generation Soviet Submarine Launched Ballistic Missiles – R-11FM, R-13 & R-21	5
3	Second Generation Soviet Submarine Launched Ballistic Missiles – R-27, R-27U, R-27K & R-29/D	39
4	Third Generation Soviet/Russian Submarine Launched Ballistic Missiles	73
5	Fourth Generation Russian Submarine Launched Ballistic Missiles	127
6	Appendices	159
7	Glossary	164

INTRODUCTION

In 2017, the sea based element of the Russian Federation nuclear deterrent triad was well advanced in its modernisation with the introduction of Project 955 Borey Strategic Missile Carrier submarines armed with the RMS-56 Bulava submarine launched ballistic missile. The Project 955/Bulava was introduced as a replacement for the Project 677BDR Strategic Missile Carrier submarines armed with R-29RKU-1/2 ballistic missiles and the Project 667BDRM Strategic Missile Carrier submarines armed with R-29RMU1/2/2.1 ballistic missiles. The Project 677BDR was on the verge of retirement whilst the Project 667BDRM was set to serve, in reducing numbers, well into the third decade of the twenty first century and possibly beyond, with an upper out of service date of 2030. The sole operational Project 941U Akula Heavy Ballistic Missile (Submarine) Cruiser remained in service in an operational/trials role with no out of service date announced by the Ministry of Defence of the Russian Federation.

    The Russian Federation was the major successor state from the dissolution of the Soviet Union in December 1991. This latter state introduced the world's first submarine launched ballistic missile and submarine based ballistic missile platform to service in 1959, sowing the seeds for four plus generations of missile submarines in Soviet and latter Russian Federation service. It was not, however, until the introduction of the Project 667A, armed, from 1968, with R-27 ballistic missile, that such submarine platforms began to be referred to as Strategic Missile Carriers. The Project 667A was the template for four more Strategic Missile Carrier designs – the Project 667B/BD/BDR/BDRM armed with increasingly capable intercontinental range ballistic missiles of the R-29/R/RK/RM series. These systems were, from 1983, augmented by the Project 941/U Heavy Ballistic Missile (Submarine) Cruisers armed with the R-39/U – the largest and most powerful ballistic missile ever fielded on a submarine launch platform.

    This volume sets out to document the four generations of Soviet and later Russian Federation submarine launched ballistic missiles carried on the four generations of conventional and nuclear powered ballistic missiles submarines that have served the Soviet and Russian Federation Northern and Pacific fleets since 1959. All technical and historical information has been furnished by the respective design bureaus, manufacturers and the Ministry of Defence of the Russian Federation with additional input from western intelligence agencies.

1

A NEW CONCEPT IN STRATEGIC STRIKE

In the decade or so following the end of World War II in 1945, a period that encompassed the early Cold War years, the USSR (Union of Soviet Socialist Republics) began to rebuild her surface and sub-surface fleets in the face of the perceived threat from the major western powers. While the Soviets were in a position of comparative weakness in regards to the naval surface forces of the major western powers, she was in a stronger position in regards to her underwater forces. The attack submarine force, still oriented for operations near Soviet shores, was being developed for enhanced open ocean operations. It was this evolution of the submarine fleets from a predominantly littoral to an open ocean force that would lead to consideration of the submarine as a weapon to threaten distant NATO (North Atlantic Treaty Organisation) nations, in particular the United States, with nuclear counter-strike. To facilitate this also required an evolution of submarine based weapons capability from the then current torpedo, mine and cruise missile (from 1956-57 the Soviets operated submarines armed with anti-ship cruise missiles).

The Soviets were heavily invested in the development of ballistic missile technology to further their offensive/defensive capabilities and for potential space exploration. The success of early ballistic missiles, despite their short range, was not lost on Soviet planners whom decreed that such weapons should be developed for operation from maritime platforms. The submarine emerged as the favoured choice due to its inherent ability to approach an enemy's shores with much reduced risk of detection in compression to a surface vessel. This view had emerged from studies, which showed that both power blocks would become increasingly reliant on sea based platforms as part of their nuclear deterrent forces. While the major NATO powers continued on the path of aircraft carrier strike forces as the major composition of their respective naval fleets, the USSR developed the submarine as the major fleet strike platform, future aircraft carrying vessels being viewed as assets whose role was to support the submarine fleets, in particular the new weapon systems what emerge as the SSB/SSBN (conventional/nuclear powered ballistic missile submarine) fleets that would be built up from 1959 through the 1980's.

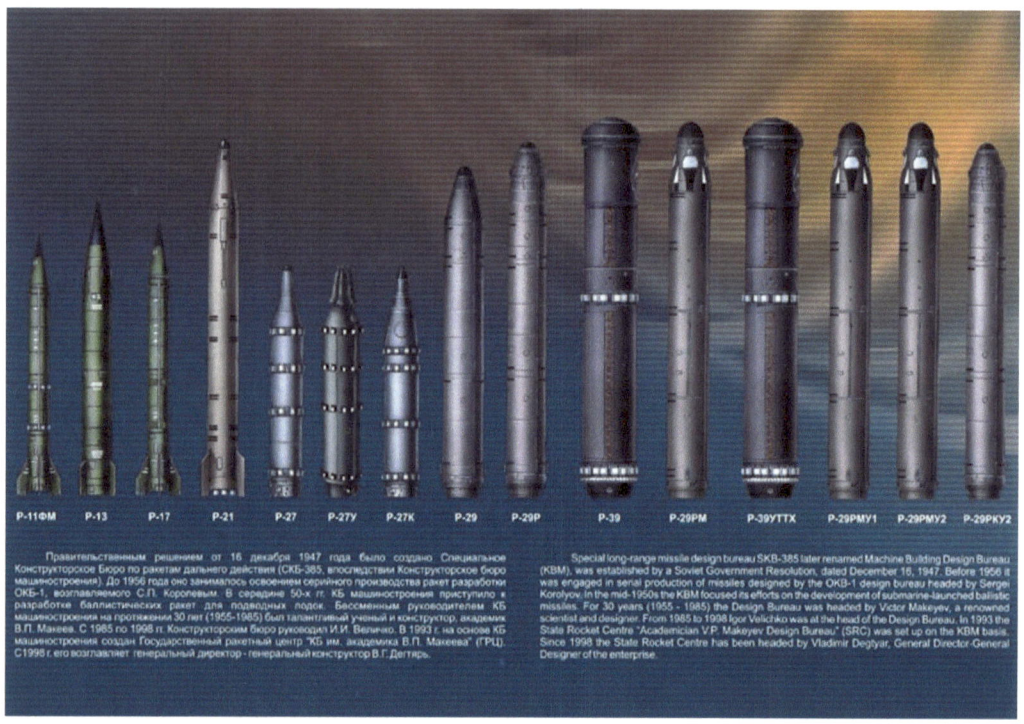

The chart above depicts three plus generations of Soviet/Russian submarine launched ballistic missile development, commencing with the R-11FM, R-13 and R-21 of the first generation, followed by the R-27, R-27U, R-27K, R-29 and R-29R of the second generation and the R-39, R-29RM, R-39UTTH, R-29RMU1, R-29RMU2 and R-29RKU1 of the third and third plus (fourth generation). KBHimmash

The changing geo-military landscape brought about by the increasing capabilities of ballistic missiles would bring about changes to the projected primary roles of the Soviet navy in the mid to late 1950's. This was a time that would witness the birth of the ballistic missile armed submarine, initially diesel-electric powered and later nuclear powered. These vessels would be armed with what would become known as the SLBM (Submarine Launched Ballistic Missile).

Although early ballistic missiles launched form first generation conventional powered ballistic missile submarines were very short on range (the submarine would have to approach to within 150 km of the enemy coast even for operations against coastal cities) they bestowed upon the Soviet Union a quantum leap in counter offensive capability. Prior to the introduction of the SSB armed with ballistic missiles the Soviet Union's primary means of reaching targets in the continental United States had been with manned bombers armed primarily with free fall nuclear bombs. The Soviets had introduced the world's first ICBM (Inter-Continental Ballistic Missile) in the shape of the OKB-1 R-7A (this weapon system achieved an operational capability in August 1957) some two years before the operational capability of the R-11FM submarine launched ballistic missile carried on the Project AB611 SSB, although ICBM's were initially intended for deployment only an a small scale.

As it had been with the first Soviet land based ballistic missiles, OKB-1 was responsible for design of the Soviet Union, and the world's, first submarine launched ballistic missile. However, following the commencement of flight testing the responsibility for major design of the missile, which emerged as the R-11FM, was handed over to SKB-385 (now JSC Company 'Academician V. P. Makeyev State Rocket Centre). This design house would go on to design no less than eight separate base SLBM complexes with a further sixteen modifications, the last of which entered service with the Russian Federation in 2012. These four generations of submarine launched ballistic missiles would serve the Soviet and later Russian navies on three generations of SSB/SSBN, three of the latter designs remaining in service with the Russian Federation Navy in 2017.

There were, of course, other design houses involved in submarine launched ballistic missile development, notably KB Arsenal, which developed the R-31 missile that would be carried on the single Project 667AM submarine. In the twenty first century the RSM-56 Bulava submarine launched ballistic missile, designed by the Moscow Institute of Thermal Technology and carried on Project 955/A/B Strategic Missile Carriers, is replacing older generation missiles of the R-29RKU/RMU/R-39U families carried on Project 667BDR, Project 667BDRM and Project 941U Strategic Missile Carrier submarines respectively.

Although intelligence agencies were reporting on Soviet submarines armed with ballistic missiles for several years prior, it was not until the occasion of the launch of the USS *John Marshall* Polaris missile armed SSBN in July 1961 that the US government became fully aware how far ahead the Soviets were in terms of number of ballistic missile submarines in service. This was itself of less importance than the realisation that the western powers had trailed so far behind the Soviets in the deployment of ballistic missiles for carriage on submarines. The following text is taken from the document 'Memorandum for the President – 22 July 1961 - Soviet statement with respect to their nuclear propelled rocket submarines':

'On 21 July [1961] the Soviet press, in commenting upon the Attorney General's speech on the occasion of the launching of the John Marshall Polaris Submarine, stated that the Soviet Union also has a nuclear submarine armed with powerful rockets of various types – submarines not inferior in speed to the American but faster. The Soviet Union has more and not less of them, in a word, the required number.

For several years now the intelligence Community has estimated that the Soviets were engaged in a major program of constructing nuclear and ballistic missile submarines; the latter we estimated, being both conventional and nuclear powered.

On 18 July, in briefing the Stennis Preparedness Subcommittee of the Armed Services Committee of the Senate, I summarized the view of the Intelligence Community with regard to the Soviet nuclear submarines program as follows: There is strong evidence of an extensive Soviet nuclear submarine building program. It is estimated that about a half dozen units are now operational, based in the Murmansk area. The combined building rate at Northern Fleet and Far

Eastern ship-yards is about seven per year. In the future, some nuclear submarines will probably carry missiles to be launched submerged, which we believe could become available in about two years.

Further, in discussing Soviet ballistic missile submarines, both conventional or possibly nuclear powered, I stated to the Subcommittee, "We recently identified a new class of long-range submarines designated H-class with 'sails' [conning tower] resembling the G-class". I added that this H-class of Soviet submarine was apparently unconventionally propelled, possibly with a nuclear power plant.

We have estimated that the present ballistic missiles carried by both the conventional and nuclear powered submarines would probably now have a maximum range up to 350 nautical miles and would have to be launched while the submarine was on the surface. Observations indicate that the H-class submarine which is apparently their first nuclear powered class [the Project 627 attack submarine was the Soviet Union's first nuclear powered submarine class], are probably somewhat smaller than the U.S. Polaris Submarines, approximately 250-290 feet in length'.

The US would, of course, have taken some comfort in the fact that the nuclear powered US SSBN's armed with sixteen 1000 km plus range Polaris missiles, which could be launched submerged, were more capable than their Soviet counterparts (although this would do nothing to remove the missile threat the US now faced). This would, however, be a temporary measure as the Soviets would counter with the deployment of the sixteen ballistic missile armed Project 667A, setting the pace for a SSBN/SLBM arms race that, it was clear, could only be countered by an arms control agreement between the opposing power blocks of East and West. This, together with the indelible fact that nuclear armed ballistic missiles were never used in anger, perhaps, being the SLBM/ballistic missile armed submarine and, indeed, the land based ICBM, greatest achievement during the high stakes games of brinkmanship played out during that most dangerous of times in human history – the late Cold War period covering the 1980's.

2

FIRST GENERATION SOVIET SUBMARINE LAUNCHED BALLISTIC MISSILES - R-11FM, R-13 & R-21

In the early 1950's, the first hypothetical paving stones were laid on the road that would lead to the SLBM (Submarine Launched Ballistic Missile) SSB/SSBN (conventional powered ballistic missile submarine/nuclear powered ballistic missile submarine) weapon system that would become a cornerstone of nuclear deterrent and counterforce nuclear strike capability during the mid and late Cold War years, and, in SLBM/SSBN form, continue in such a capacity in the second decade of the twenty first century.

The USSR (Union of Soviet Socialist Republics) had become the world's second nuclear power in 1949, but, through the 1950's struggled to counter NATO (North Atlantic Treaty Organisation) overwhelming nuclear weapon delivery capability. In pursuit of this she turned to a new weapon system, the SLBM/SSB, as a means to providing a high degree of certainty in being able to deliver at least a small number of nuclear warheads against United States cities in the hope that this would dissuade the NATO against any endeavour to attack the Soviet Union with nuclear weapons. The submarine launched ballistic missiles would form part of a planned triad of nuclear deterrent forces, which, in the mid-1950's, centred on long-range aviation bombers and land-based IRBM (Intermediate Range Ballistic Missiles), the latter lacking sufficient range to target the continental United States proper. Within a few years the Soviet's would introduce a fledgling ICBM (Inter-Continental Ballistic Missile) force to their nuclear deterrent triad, although it would be a decade or so before this would constitute the major part of that nation's nuclear strike forces.

The doorway to the SLBM was opened with a Soviet government decree, issued on 26 January 1954, calling for the development of sea platform, primarily submarine, launched ballistic missiles able to strike an aggressor state. Prior to this, on 14 July 1953, OKB-1 had outlined technical requirements for a new missile, the R-11FM, which would be developed from the land-based R-11 SRBM (Short-Range Ballistic Missile that would itself lead to the R-17 SRBM). There was a meeting of chief designers on 5 January 1954, OKB-1 chief designer, S. P. Korolev, heading the program with I. V. Popkova appointed leading designer. One of the decisions taken was to develop a test complex (apparently designed in collaboration by S. P. Korolev, N. Isanin and E. G. Rudyak) centered on a test stand that could be used to simulate sea-based ballistic missile launches. Other decisions taken were to design a missile launch complex that would not require deep redesign of a submarine structure, in this case the chosen platform being the Project 611 diesel-electric attack submarine.

The R-11FM (above) was a maritime based development of the R-11 ballistic missile (itself evolving into the R-17 ballistic missile). Makeyev

For launch the missile would be raised through the modified conning tower (sail) (conning tower) of the Project 611 submarine until the major part of the missile structure was protruding. It would be held in a raised vertical position by a launch hold system designed by A. P. Abramov of OKB-1. Initial test launches, numbering twelve, were conducted from the 'stand' complex. This phase included launches of missiles with a redesigned control-system. The next stage involved launches from a 'rocking stand' complex designed to simulate launches from a submarine pitching in the sea. The R-11FM control system was designed to have navigation data uploaded prior to launch, taking into consideration the pitch of the sea, which would have an obvious effect on missile trajectory at launch and, thus, terminal phase accuracy.

During September and October 1954, three R-11FM missiles were launched from fixed land-based launch platforms, allowing the basic missile technicalities to be proven. These initial launches were followed by R-11FM test launches from the swinging bench platform to simulate a launch from a pitching submarine, the first of this series of launches being conducted on 25 May 1955, with the concluding launch of the series being conducted on 30 July that year. The test stand was designed to demonstrate the raising of the missile through the conning tower to the launch position and the subsequent launch in a number of sea states. For this the stand could be moved in roll and yaw, up to 12° in the former and 4° in the latter, simulating launch in sea states up to 4. There were eleven launches during this phase, nine of which reached the designated target areas, which, at its farthest, was 240 km from the launch point.

Russian/Soviet Submarine Launched Ballistic Missiles

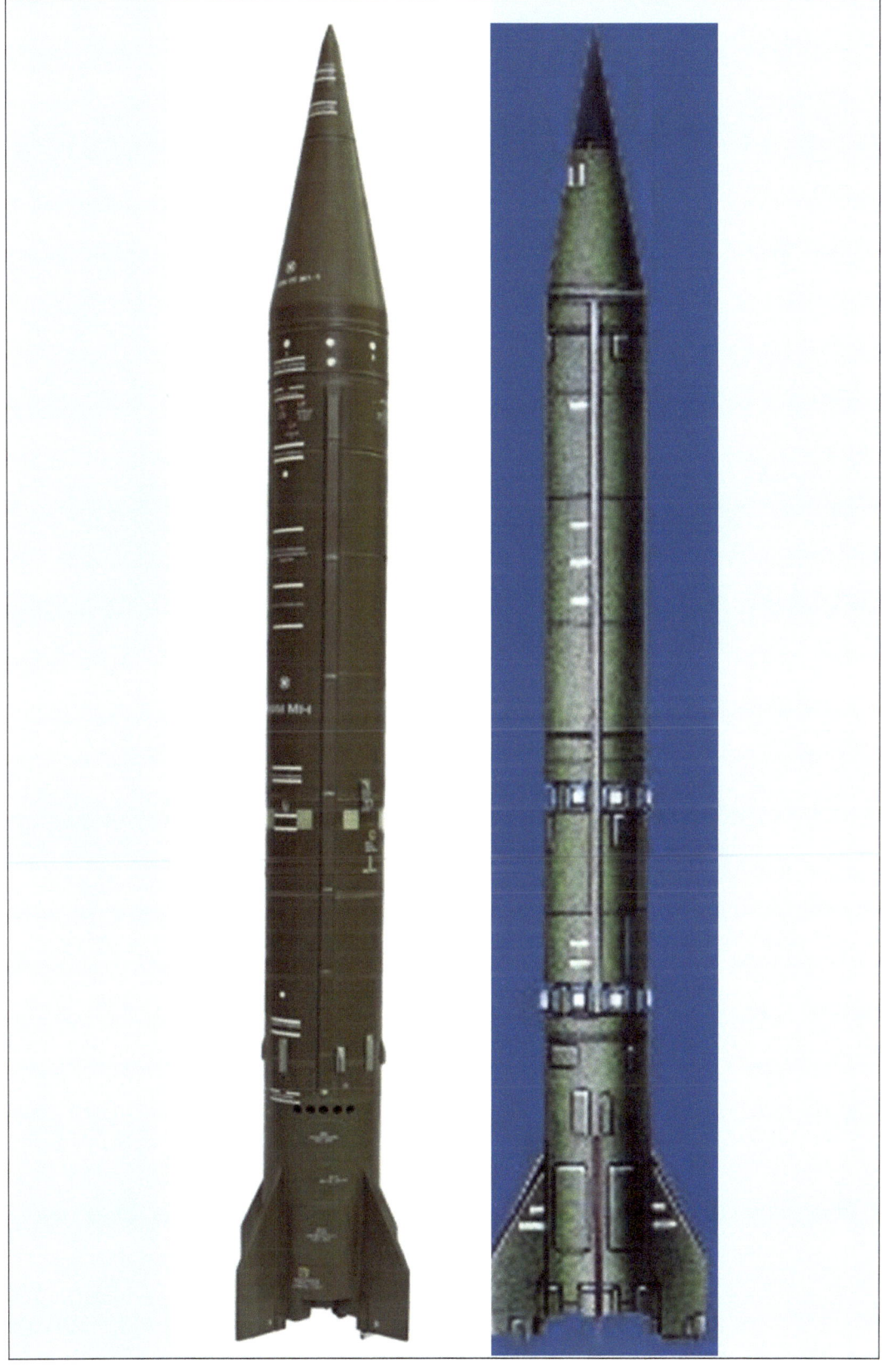

Page 7: Two slightly different rotated views of the R-11FM (both graphics are to slightly different scales). Page 8: Russian language graphic depicting the various compartments of the R-11FM missile. Text reproduced below with English translation non-bolded in parenthesis: **неотделяемая головная часть** (inseparable head part); **оссек приборов системы управления и системы подачи топлива** (axis of control system and fuel supply system); **бак окислителя** (oxidizer tank); **оссек приборов системы управления и системы подачи топлива** (axis of control system and fuel supply system); **опоры, воспринимающие нагрузку от пусковой установки (показаны условно)** (supports that receive load from the launcher (shown conditionally)); **труба подвода окислителя** (oxidant supply pipe); **бак горючего** (fuel tank); **однокамерный двигатель** (single-chamber engine); **хвостовой отсек** (tail section); **стабилизаторы** (stabilizers); **газовые рули** (gas controlled rudders). **This page: The single reentry vehicle nuclear warhead of the R-11FM.** Makeyev

The successful conclusion of the R-11FM test phases cleared the way for sea trials on a Project 611 (NATO reporting name 'Zulu') submarine that had been modified to Project AV611 standard. Rubin Design Bureau (Central Design Bureau Rubin) had produced the basic technical design for the Project 611 large ocean going diesel electric submarine in 1948. B-61, the first boat of this class, which was developed under chief designer S. A. Egorov, was commissioned into the Soviet Navy in 1953, twenty six boats being built.

The Project 611 design was subsequently used as the basis for Project 641/641B Ocean going diesel electric submarines and the Project 627, the first Soviet nuclear powered submarine. Five standard torpedo armed Project 611 attack submarines were converted to full AV611 configuration (some NATO assessments state 6-7 conversions, but PA Sevmash (Plant No.402) writings indicate that only five boats were put in full operational service) that allowed them to carry two R-11FM missiles, housed in a modified conning tower, and launch them while on the ocean surface.

Previous page: R-11FM missiles are raised to their lunch positon atop the conning tower of an AV611 SSB. This page: R-11FM ballistic missiles launched from an AV611 SSB. US NHC/PA Sevmash/Energia

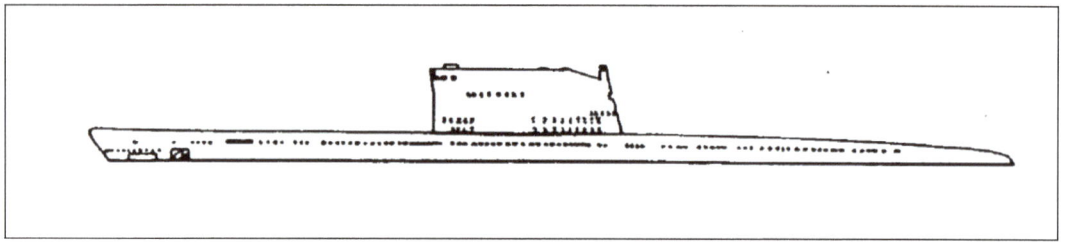

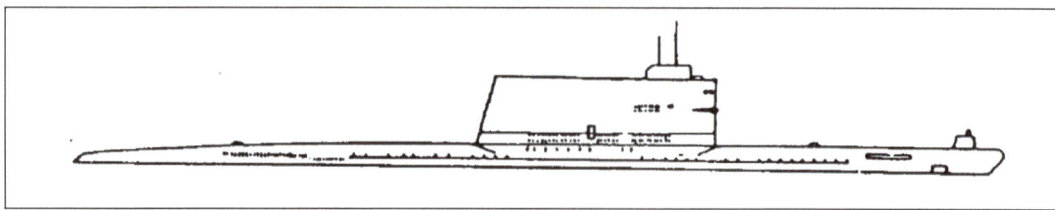

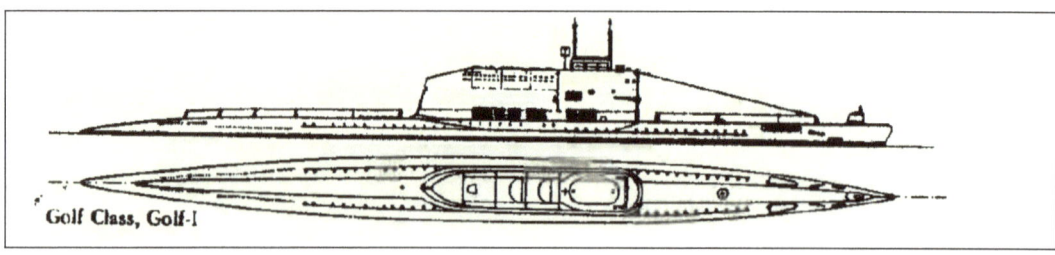

Top: An operational AV611 submarine in service with the Soviet Navy in the early 1960's. Upper centre: Starboard side profile drawing of an unmodified Project 611 ('Zulu' class), from which the AV611 was developed. Centre: Port side profile drawing of the basic outline of the AV611 SSB. Lower centre: Starboard side profile drawing of the basic outline of the Project 629 SSB. Above: Detailed starboard side and plan view drawing of the Project 629A 'Golf' I. Makeyev/USNHC/US Gov

This image purports to show an R-11FM missile being loaded aboard a Project 629A ('Golf' I) SSB. However, conflicting data suggests the possibility that it may be an R-13 ballistic missile, the stabilizer design being indicative of the R-13 design. Makeyev

In August 1955, as the program team was preparing for a test launch from an AV611 submarine, development of the R-11FM was transferred from OBK-1 to SKB-385, retaining considerable OKB-1 support. Amidst the bureaucratic and administrative changes, the development team pressed ahead with work to clear the missile for the submarine launch phase of the trials. On 16 September 1955, an R-11FM ballistic missile was launched from the modified Project AV611 submarine, B-67 (commanded by Captain 2nd Rank F. I. Kozlov), whilst the vessel was on the surface in the White Sea. Onboard the submarine was a technical team that included the head of OKB-1, S. P. Korolev. This successful launch, which occurred at 17.32 hours local time, effectively heralded the beginning of the era of ballistic missile submarines that continues in the second decade of the twenty first century.

This initial launch from a submarine was followed by further launches that included a single launch from a ground-based swinging stand and five more launches conducted from the AV611. These development test launches were followed by operational testing with the Soviet Northern Fleet (Makeyev documentation states the Northern and Pacific Fleets, but Energia documentation refers only to the Northern Fleet) during August and October 1956. This phase, which involved the launch of R-11FM missiles from four operational AV611 SSB's, included launches of

R-11FM missiles after varying periods of storage. The first such launch, which was conducted at 10.01 hours on 12 September 1956, utilised R-11FM missile S.2-10, which had been in storage for 37 days. Two R-11FM's were launched on 3 October 1956, the first, S.2-2, at 10.31 hours after having been in storage for 82 days and the second, R-11FM S.2-12, being launched at 14.02 hours after 47 days in storage.

The last phase of development testing involved a series of four R-11FM missile launches during the course of March-May 1958. Three of these launches were successful, and one, conducted in April, was unsuccessful due to a leak in a pipeline. Despite the failure, the three successful launches had provided validation of the R-11FM/AV611 weapon system, paving the way for the complex to be put forward for operational deployment (two R-11FM missiles being accommodated in the modified conning tower) officially entering service with the Soviet Navy in a surface launch capacity on 20 February 1959. The R-11FM would go on to constitute the nuclear strike armament of not only the Project AV611 SSB, but also the Project 629 (NATO reporting name 'Golf', later classified 'Golf' I) class SSB. As late as 1969, western intelligence agencies believed that the weapon formed the armament of some nuclear powered 'Hotel' (later classified 'Hotel' I) class submarines, although this assessment was erroneous.

The AV611 had been a crash program in order to achieve the earliest possible operational capability for a ballistic missile armed submarine as a partial counter balance to NATO's growing nuclear strike capability. However, as the AV611/R-11FM programs were progressing, design studies led to the authorisation for two purpose designed missile platforms, the diesel-electric powered Project 629 SSB and the nuclear powered Project 658 SSBN - unlike the Project 658, the Project 629 would initially be armed with the R-11FM. A total of sixteen Project 629/B missile submarines (NATO reporting names 'Golf' (later 'Golf' I) & 'Golf' II) were built by PA Sevmash in Severodvinsk (Soviet North West) between 1959 and 1962, with seven others being built at Komsomolsk on Amur in the Soviet Far East. Three R-11FM missiles could be carried by the Project 629, the sixteen vessels joining five operational Project AV611 submarines (at least one other V/AV611 was apparently utilised for test purposes) that preceded them.

Often overlooked, NATO intelligence assessments often attributed the SS-N-4 prefix to the R-11FM. This reporting prefix was later carried over to the R-13 missile. As late as May 1969, US intelligence reports considered that the SS-N-4 had attained an operational capability sometime in 1960, it being unclear if this estimate was applicable to the R-11FM or R-13, the former having been operational since the previous year, as noted above. Late 1960's NATO intelligence assessments for the range of the SS-N-4, at 150 km, were accurate if applied to the R-11FM, but considerably short if applied to the R-13. Intelligence assessments were accurate in their consideration that guidance was inertial, this being typical of the time. In regards to CEP (Circular Error Probability), western intelligence agencies estimated the SS-N-4 at 1-2 nm (1.9-3.7 km), Soviet values being in the region of 1.5 km for the warhead, which western intelligence estimated, with reasonable accuracy, as being in the region of 2,200 lb. (997 kg). Soviet values for actual weight class were slightly lower.

R-11FM – data furnished by OJSC Makeyev State Rocket Centre and S. P. Korolev Rocket and Space Corporation, Energia

Launch mass: 5.5 tons (S. P. Korolev Rocket and Space Corporation, Energia states 5440 kg)
Weight of empty missile: 2047 kg
Weight of rocket fuel components
    Nitric acid AK-20I and kerosene T-1, a mixture of TG-02, gas: 3393 kg
Traction control on the ground: 8260 kg
Specific impulse control at sea level: 218 kgf/s/kg
Length: 10.3 m
Diameter: 0.88 m
Number of stages: 1
Control system: inertial
Type of reentry vehicle: single reentry vehicle
Weight of warhead: 967 kg
Maximum firing range: 150 km
Probable deviations from the target: ± 1.5 km in range and ± 0.75 km lateral
Force of sea for missile launch: up to 4-5
Carrier vessel: Project AV611 and Project 629
Number of missiles carried by submarine: 2 (Project AV611) and 3 (Project 629)

The project AV611 (above) and some Project 629 ('Golf' I) submarines were armed with the R-11FM, other Project 629's being armed with the larger, more powerful and longer range R-13. The R-13, as was the case with the R-11FM/AV611, was hoisted atop the conning tower of the Project 629 and launched in a similar fashion to that of the R-11FM. Makeyev

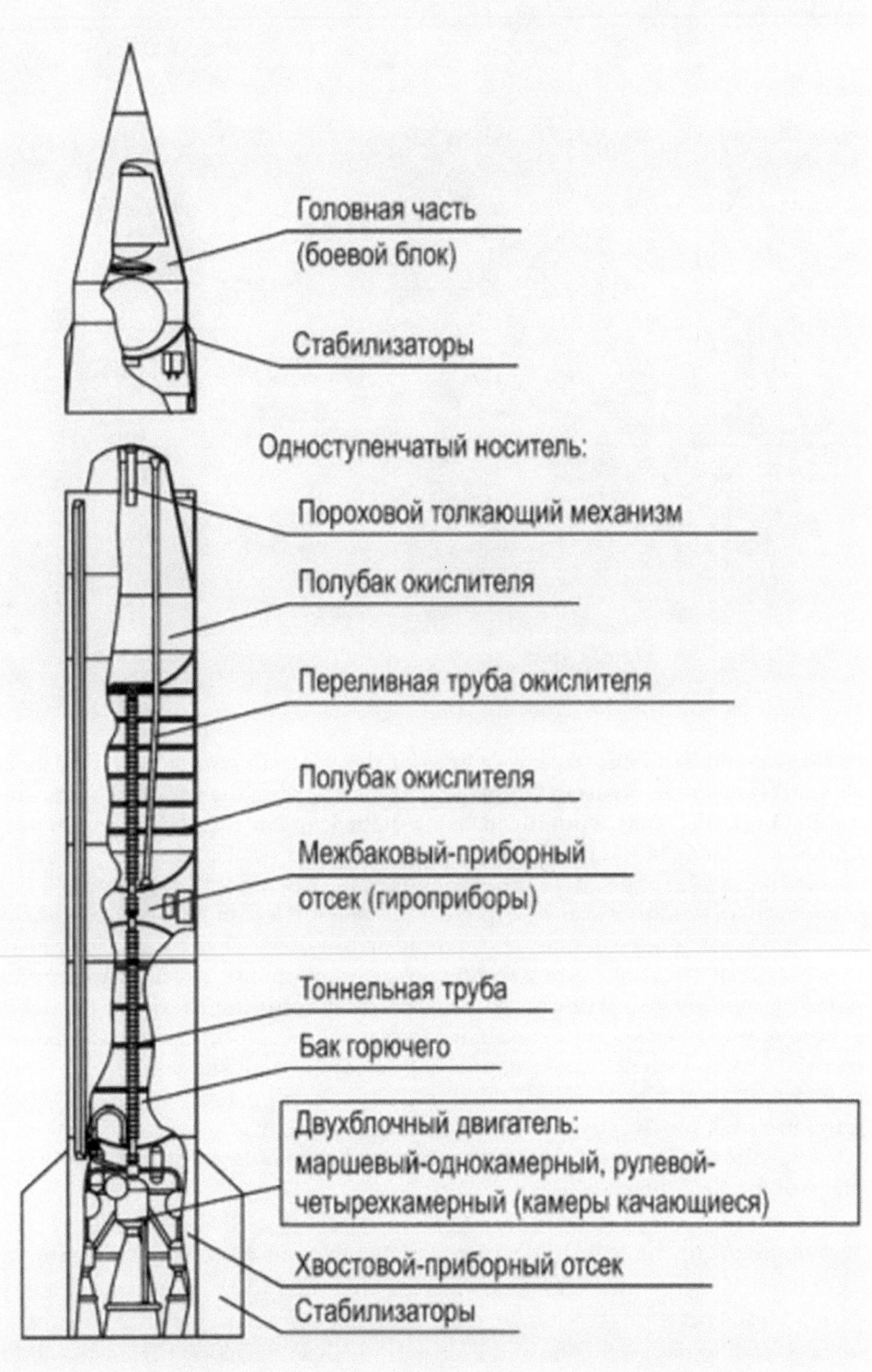

Page 16: Graphic depicting the outer lines of the R-13 submarine launched ballistic missile. Previous page: Russian language graphic showing the various compartments of the R-13 missile. Text reproduced below with English translation non-bolded in parenthesis): головная часть (боевой блок) (head part combat block (unit) [warhead]); **стабилизаторы** (stabilizers); **одноступенчатый носитель** (single-stage carrier); **пороховой толкающий механизм** (powder pushing mechanism); **полубак окислителя** (half oxidizing agent); **переливная труба окислителя** (oxidizer overflow pipe); **полубак окислителя** (half oxidizing agent); **межбаковый-приборный отсек (гироприборы)** (inter-tank instrument compartment (gyro-equipment)); **тоннельная труба** (tunnel pipe); **бак горючего** (fuel tank); **двухблочный двигатель** (two block engine); **двухблочный двигатель маршевый-однокамерный, рулевой-четырехкамерный (камеры качающиеся)** (two block engine, single chamber, steering four chambers (swaying)); **хвостовой-приборный отсек** (tail instrument compartment) **стабилизаторы** (stabilizers). **Above: The re-entry vehicle shell and the warhead casing for the single warhead of the R-13 missile.** Makeyev

Development of the R-13 (D-2 complex), which was allocated the technological index reference 4K-50 (this complex was allocated the NATO reporting designation SS-N-4), commenced in 1956 under chief designer Makeyev, with L.M. Miloslavsky appointed leading designer. The single-stage R-13 was developed from the R-11FM to address the formers shortcoming in range, retaining the single-stage configuration of its forbear.

The thermonuclear warhead of the R-13 had a yield ~50 times greater than that of the R-11FM nuclear warhead. Makeyev

R-13 test launches from a submarine platform were conducted during 1959-1960, paving the way for the weapon system to enter service in the latter year following the winding up of the first phase operational flight testing of the R-11FM. The R-13 had a launch weight 2.5 times that of the R-11FM, but was able to fly in the region of four times farther. The change from a nuclear to thermonuclear warhead, the latter developed by a collaboration of SKB-385 and NII-1011 of the Ministry of Medium Machine Building, increased warhead weight by a factor of 1.5, but was considered a quantum leap forward as warhead yield was ~50 times greater than that achieved with the R-11FM nuclear charge. On 20 October 1961, an R-13 missile, launched from a submarine, impacted the Novaya Zemlya range in the near Arctic North–central Russia, with an explosive force equivalent to 1,450 tons of TNT, demonstrating the enormous destructive power of the weapon.

Page 20, 21 and 22: The first platform to be armed with operational R-13 missiles was the diesel-electric submarines of the Project 629(A) ('Golf') class. USNHC

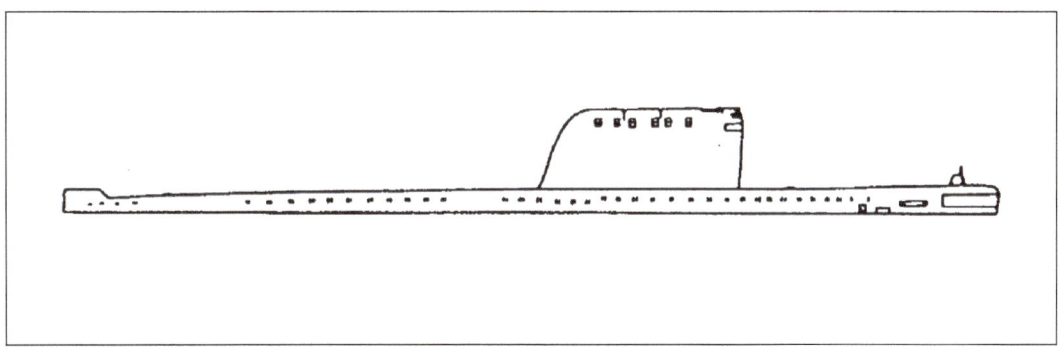

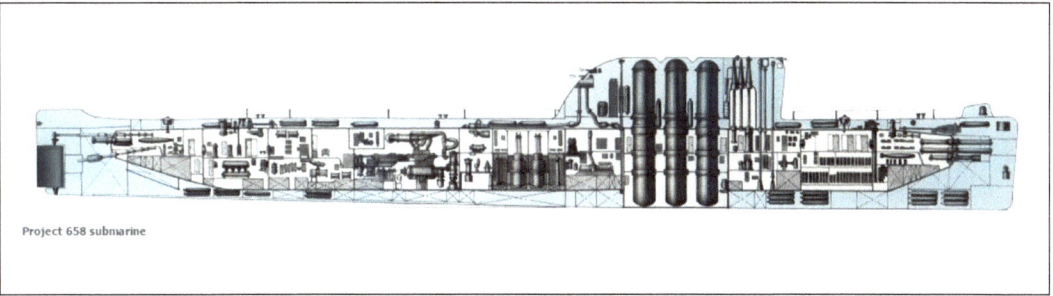

This page top: Starboard side profile drawing showing the basic outline of the nuclear powered Project 658 ('Hotel', later coded 'Hotel' I) class ballistic missile submarine. Above: Starboard side view diagram of the nuclear powered Project 658 ballistic missile submarine showing the arrangement of the three single-stage submarine launched ballistic missiles housed in the conning tower (sail). This arrangement was similar to that on the Project 629 diesel-electric powered ballistic missile carrying submarine. USNHC/CDB-Rubin

The R-13 would arm the Project 629 series diesel-electric ballistic missile submarine (three missiles accommodated) and the Project 658 (allocated the NATO reporting name 'Hotel') nuclear powered ballistic missile submarine (three missiles accommodated). Research and development on the first generation of nuclear powered ballistic missile submarines had commenced at CDB-Rubin in 1956, sowing the seeds for four generations of ballistic missile boats, all of which Rubin had the lead design role. The Project 658(M), designed under the leadership of S.N. Kovalev, was developed as the Soviet Union's first nuclear powered ballistic missile carrying submarine, almost in concert with the first Soviet designed nuclear powered submarine, the Project 627 attack submarine designed at the Malachite Design Bureau - the first Project 627 was handed over to the Soviet Navy in 1958. Eight Project 658 nuclear submarines were built between 1960 and 1962 (CDB-Rubin states that Project 658 boats were built between 1960-1964, this probably reflecting the service delivery years). When the lead Project 658 submarine, K-19 (built by PA Sevmash at Severodvinsk), joined the Soviet navy in 1960, it introduced a quantum leap in the Soviet nuclear counterstrike capability by allowing the submarine to stay submerged during an entire patrol, with the exception of having to surface to launch its trio of R-13 missiles, should this become necessary.

The Project 658 'Hotel' class had a distinctive profile with its forward sloping trailing end on the conning tower. US DoD

R-13 (D-2 complex) – data furnished by OJSC Makeyev State Rocket Centre

Launch mass: 13.6 tons
Length: 11.8 m
Diameter: 1.3 m
Number of stages: 1
Fuel: liquid
Control system: inertial
Type of reentry vehicle: single reentry vehicle
Firing range: 600 km
Force of sea: up to 4-5
Carrier vessel: Project 629 and Project 658
Number of missiles carried by submarine: 3

R-13 missiles launches from a Project 629 submarine (top) and from a Project 658 submarine (above). Makeyev/PA Sevmash

The R-11FM (D-1 complex) SLBM arming Project AV611 and Project 629 SSB's had a range of only 150 km, requiring these vessels to patrol very close to a potential enemy's coastlines, primarily the East and West coasts of the United States, with all the hazards that this entailed. The introduction of the 600 km range R-13 (D-2 complex) arming later Project 629 SSB and the nuclear powered Project 658 SSBN improved the situation considerably. However, patrol areas were still too close to the United States coasts for realistic support to be afforded by Soviet surface combatants (including the later Project 1123 ASW (Anti-Submarine Warfare) helicopter carriers - *Moskva* was commissioned on 25 December 1967). There could be no great confidence of support from shore based maritime patrol/ASW aircraft (including same operating from Cuba ~165 km from Florida on the United States East Coast), which would have been extremely vulnerable to American anti-air defenses.

In regards to submarine vulnerability on having to surface to launch ballistic missiles, it should be considered that the overriding priority would be the launch of the missiles, not the safety of the submarine afterwards. Once the missiles were in flight the submarine would have been considered to have successfully carried out its primary mission of nuclear counterstrike against a nuclear aggressor. It seems implausible to consider that the fifteen or twenty minutes required for this task would have been unattainable. On the contrary, there was a high probability that a submarine that had not been detected prior to surfacing for missile launch in an area with no ASW assets in the immediate vicinity would, with a high degree of confidence, be able to launch its missiles and submerge again before being subjected to attack. This assessment in no way glosses over the inherent vulnerability of submarine platforms when operating near the coasts of the respective opposing power blocks of East and West. However, it should be born in mind that around 85% of NATO's West Atlantic ASW assets were deployed during the Cuban Missile Crisis of October/November 1962 (data sourced from USN intelligence department). These ASW assets detected only three of the four Soviet Project 641 F (NATO reporting name 'Foxtrot') Class submarines of the 69th Brigade, 20th Submarine Squadron (this squadron included a division of Project 629 ballistic missile submarines, the deployment of which to Cuba was cancelled) deployed to the Sea of Saragossa (vicinity of the Bahama's) under operation 'Kama', the naval element of operation 'Anadyr'. One of those submarines was discovered because it was unserviceable, and, on being returned to serviceability following repairs at sea, submerged under the noses of its attendant NATO ASW vessels and slipped away. Contact was not reestablished, the submarine, not only remaining undetected, but going on to track an American Helicopter Carrier, apparently the USS *Thetis Bay*, until ordered home. This operation, while lauded as a success for NATO in its confrontation with the Soviets, was, to a degree, a successful operation for the small deployed Soviet submarine force, this fact being lost on a Soviet leadership furious that any of its submarines had been discovered at all. It should be noted that had any of the deployed submarines been nuclear powered, then there would have been no need to surface for air/battery recharging depriving NATO of its psychological victory in that it was able to broadcast images of surfaced Soviet submarines to a public infused with anti-Soviet propaganda.

There were, of course, ways to mitigate the risk to the SSB/SSBN on the surface during missile launch. For instance, the Soviets employed ASCM (Anti-Ship Cruise Missile) armed submarines. These, whilst having a primary anti-aircraft carrier task force role, could, and probably would have, to an extent, been utilised to protect SSB/SSBN's on the surface against enemy surface combatants. It would have been difficult for a Destroyer, Frigate or Corvette to initiate an attack on a submarine while this ship was itself under attack from several cruise missiles, which, in the early 1960's, were practically invulnerable to ship mounted air defence systems, particularly in adverse weather and during the hours of darkness.

Project 613 "C-146" submarine

Soviet first generation SSB/SSBN's could be provided with support from Soviet ASCM (Anti-Ship Cruise Missile) armed submarines, initially converted diesel-electric attack submarines like the C-146 conversion of the Project 613 (top) armed with P-5 ASCMs and later nuclear powered submarines of the Project 659 ('Echo' I) (above) and Project 675 ('Echo' II) armed with the P-6 ASCM complex. Both the P-5 and the P-6 were launched whilst the boats were on the surface. CDB-Rubin/US DoD

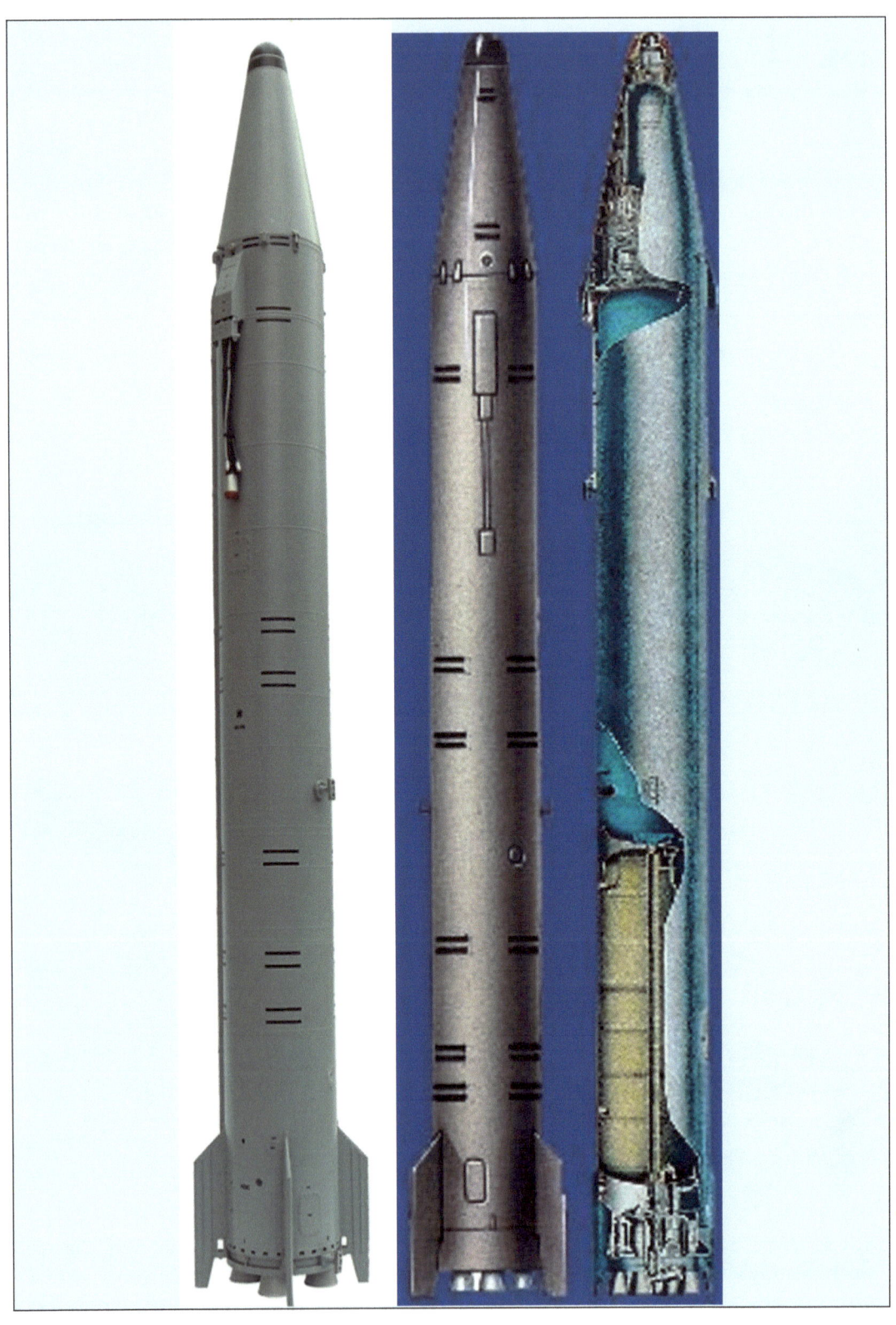

Trio of diagrams of the R-21 submarine launched ballistic missile. Makeyev

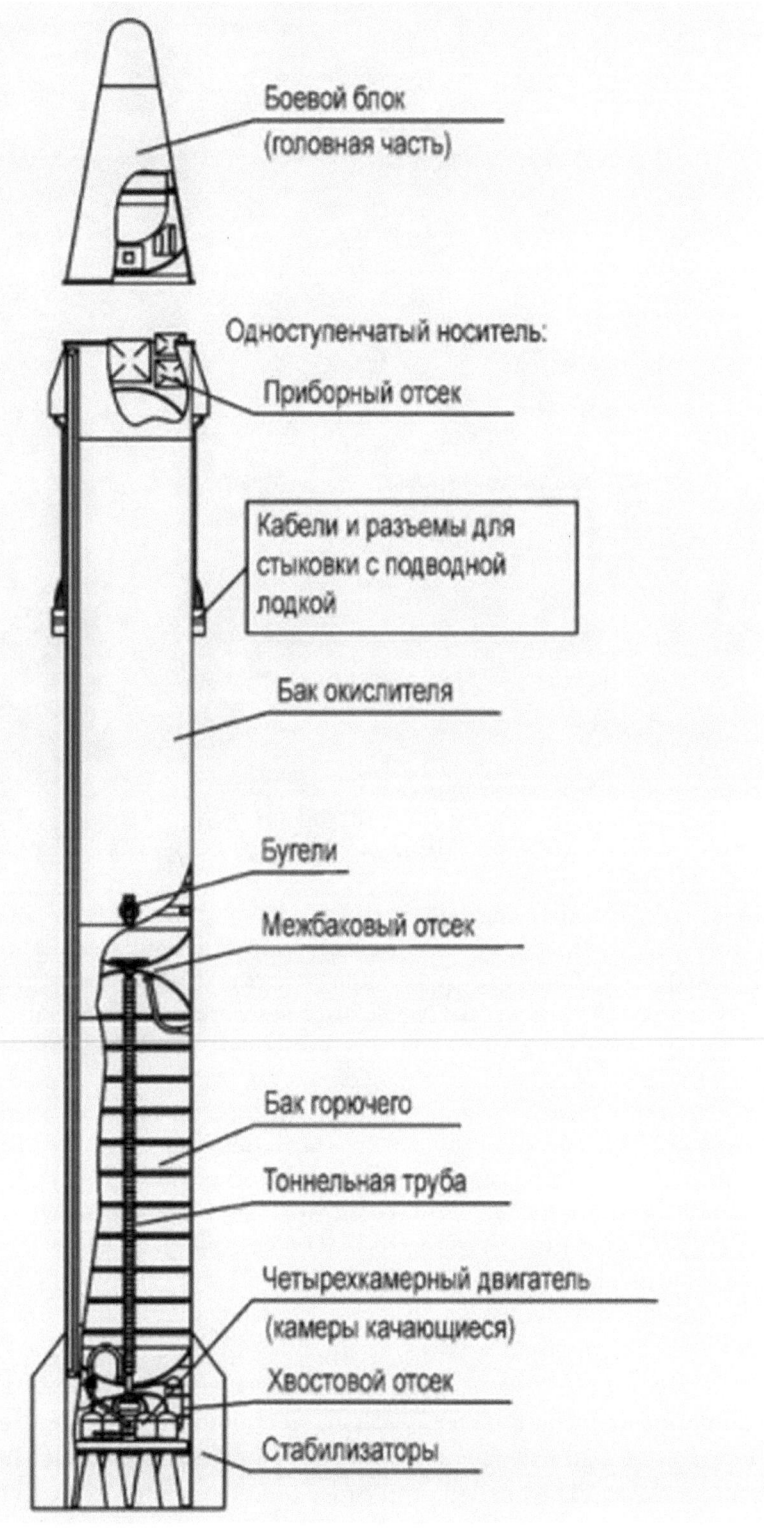

Previous page: Russian language graphic showing the various compartments of the R-21 missile. Text reproduced below with English translation non-bolded in parenthesis). боевой блок (головная часть) (combat unit (warhead head-part)); одноступенчатый носитель (single-stage carrier); приборный отсек (instrument compartment); кабели и разъемы для стысовкм с подводной лодкой (cables and connectors for docking with a submarine); бак окиспителя (oxidizer tank); бугели (bugle); межбаковыи отсек (inter-storage compartment); бак горючего (fuel tank); тоннельная труба (tunnel pipe); четыреххамерный двмгатель (камеры качающиеся) (four-dimensional (or four chamber) engine (swinging)); хвостовой отсек (tail section (compartment)); стабилизаторы (stabilizers). **Above: Elements of the rocket engine compartment of the R-21 (D-4 complex).** Makeyev

Notwithstanding the above, it was clear that a submarine that could launch its missiles whilst submerged was considerably less vulnerable than such a platform that had to surface to effect same. This was not lost on the Soviet design teams working on submarine launched ballistic missile technology. To effect such a capability, development of a sub-surface launch system for ballistic missiles had commenced in 1955 under the R-11FM program in order to address the issue of vulnerability on the sea surface for the launch platform. The first underwater launch of an R-11FM, powered by a solid-propellant engine, which replaced the liquid propellant engine, was conducted in the Black Sea on 26 December 1956, firing depth being 30 m.

Thermonuclear warhead section of the R-21 (D-4 complex). Makeyev

However, the decision was taken not to pursue a sub-surface launched variant of the R-11FM to enter production, this accord being carried over to the R-13. Instead, the decision was taken to address the short-range of the R-11FM/R-13 and the sub-surface launch question at the same time. This resulted in a new design designated R-21 (D-4 complex), allocated the Soviet technological index reference 4K-55 and the NATO reporting designation SS-N-5. Development commenced in 1959 under Makeyev with V.L. Kleiman appointed leading designer. The R-21 required smaller (in diameter) launch tubes than that required for the R-13 and featured an extended firing range of 1420 km, in the order of 2.5 times greater than that of the R-13 and 9.5 times greater than that of the R-11FM. Other than extended range, the R-21 stood apart from its forebears in that, as noted above, it was designed for sub-surface launch, removing the inherent vulnerability of the surface launched R-11FM and R-13. This reduced the vulnerability of the carrier submarine, which no longer had to surface to launch missiles. The ability to launch underwater also increased operational availability as the missiles were able to be fired from depths of 40-50 m at sea states up to 5 when the carrier submarine was travelling at speeds of up to 4 knots. From firing alert it took around 30 minutes to prepare a missile for launch, a three missile salvo able to be launched within a ten minute period.

The R-21M designation was allocated to R-21 missiles equipped with a new warhead, this variant attaining operational capability on Project 658M(B) 'Hotel' II SSBN's in 1981.

Top: Crude Profile view drawing of the Soviet 'Golf' II (Project 629B) class SSB that was armed with three R-21 (D-4 complex) submarine launched ballistic missiles, which could be launched whilst the submarine was submerged. Above: A DIA artwork depicting the submerged launch of an SS-N-5 (R-21) ballistic missile from a 'Golf' II class SSB. The Project 629B and the nuclear powered Project 658M, armed with the R-21, provided the Soviet Union with a submerged SLBM capability in advance of the initial operational capability of the Project 667A ('Yankee') class SSBN armed with the R-27 SLBM. US Gov./DIA

Previous page: Project 629B 'Golf' II class submarines on the ocean surface. This page top: A 'Golf' II submarine underway on the sea surface off the coast of Denmark with its attendant NATO shadow, the USN Frigate USS *Pharris* (FF-1094). Above: A trio of Project 629 submarines in icy waters at the Soviet Northern Fleet submarine base at Polyarny, Kola in North West Russia. USNHC/US DoD/Makeyev

An R-21 submarine launched ballistic missile launched from a submerged submarine. Makeyev

R-21 missiles would be installed on updated Project 629 diesel-electric missile submarines of the Project 629B (allocated the NATO reporting name 'Golf' II) and Project 658M(B) (NATO reporting name 'Hotel' II) nuclear powered ballistic missile submarines. Test launches were conducted in the years 1962-1963 and the complex was accepted for operational service with the Soviet Navy in the latter year.

The decision was taken to retrofit early boats of the Project 629 and 658 classes armed with surface launched missiles of the R-13 type with the improved R-21. To this end, a modification program for the Project 658 commenced in 1963. Modifications were carried out at several yards, including the Zvezdochka Shipyard in the Arkhangelsk region of Soviet Russia, repair and re-equipment of the Project 658M submarine K-33 (serial No. 902) commencing at this yard in 1965. The Zvezdochka Shipyard was also involved in the conversion of Project 629 boats to launch the R-21 missile, Project 629A submarine K-88 (serial No. 807) being so modified (to Project 629B standard) in 1966.

Previous page and above: A Project 629B 'Hotel' II submarine partially disabled some 600 miles North East of Newfoundland on 29 Feb 1972. US DoD

Western intelligence got their first close look at the R-21 when the complex made its first public appearance at a parade held in the Northern Soviet port city of Murmansk in November 1967, although there were occasional glimpses of the missile on various Soviet/East European television broadcasts for a few years prior to this. As late as summer 1969, western intelligence agencies assessed that the SS-N-5 had a firing range in the region of 650 nm (1204 km), this being slightly over 200 km short of the actual value of 1420 km. As with the NATO SS-N-4 assessment, CEP was slightly lower than the NATO assessment.

R-21 (D-4 complex) – data furnished by OJSC Makeyev State Rocket Centre

Launch mass: 19.7 tons
Length: 14.2 m
Diameter: 1.3 m
Number of stages: 1
Fuel: liquid
Control system: inertial
Type of reentry vehicle: single reentry vehicle
Firing range: 1420 km
Force of sea for missile launch: up to 5
Carrier vessel: Project 629 and Project 658
Number of missiles carried by submarine: 3

3

SECOND GENERATION SOVIET SUBMARINE LAUNCHED BALLISTIC MISSILES – R-27/R-27U/R-27K/R-29/D

From 1959 through the early 1970's the Soviet Union built up large fleets of ballistic missile submarines armed with a diversity of ballistic missile variants. The aforementioned Project AV611 and Project 629/629B SSB (conventional powered ballistic missile submarine) and Project 658M(B) SSBN (nuclear powered ballistic missile submarine) fleets were now joined by Project 677A and Project 677B SSBN's armed with R-27 and R-29 SLBM (Submarine Launched Ballistic Missiles) respectively. From its early lead over the United States, the Soviet Union, by the early 1960's, was not only facing the prospect, but was materially already falling behind the United States in terms of the operational capability of SLBM and their launch platforms, the ballistic missile submarine. In late 1960, the submerged launch capability Polaris A2 SLBM armed George Washington class SSBN (the lead vessel was commissioned in December 1959, but was not operational as a missile armed boat until November 1960) entered service, commencing the build-up of a NATO ballistic missile submarine force. This saw the United States overtake the capability of the Soviet Union's Project 629 SSB and Project 658 SSBN armed with the R-13 and (in terms of numbers of missiles carried) from 1963, the submerged launch capability R-21 SLBM.

The Project AV611 (armed with the R-11FM), Project 629 (various units armed with the R-11FM, R-13 and, from 1966, the R-21) and Project 658 (armed with the R-13 and, from 1963, the R-21) had constituted the first generation of Soviet ballistic missile submarine/SLBM. The second generation of strategic missile carrying submarines of the Project 667A class (NATO reporting name 'Yankee'), armed with the R-27 second generation SLBM, was built as a Soviet response to the US building the fleet of Polaris armed George Washington class SSBN's (this is borne out by Soviet and later Russian bureau texts that indicate same). The Project 667A, developed under chief designer S.N. Kovalev, would restore the balance and provide a platform for the Soviet Union to achieve parity with, and eventually surpass, the United States in regards to numbers and capability of its SSBN/SLBM fleets.

An early production R-27 ballistic missile undergoing shore preparation for installation on a Project 667A submarine. Makeyev

The first of thirty four Project 667A Strategic Nuclear Submarine Cruisers (twenty four built at Severodvinsk 1967-1972 and ten built at Komsomolsk-on-Amur 1969-1972), K-137, was commissioned into the Soviet Navy on 5 November 1967. This was the same year that the first of the Project 1123 Moskva Class ASW (Anti-Submarine Warfare) helicopter carrying Cruisers was commissioned. This class of vessel initially had SSBN protection as a primary role. Following operational trials K-137 achieved an operational capability with the R-27 missile, sixteen housed in launch tubes located aft of the conning tower (sail) in 1968.

It was with the introduction of the Project 667A/R-27, missile range being 2500 km, that realistic support in the general SSBN patrol areas could become a viable operational role for the Project 1123 and later the Project 1143 V/STOL (Vertical/Short Take-Off and Landing) capable aircraft carrier (initially termed ASW Cruisers with Airborne Armament), albeit still retaining significant operational risk. Such patrol areas, closer to waters more readily under Soviet guard, were more attainable with the introduction of the 3000 km range R-27U, sixteen of which were carried by the Project 667AU. By the time these weapon systems entered service a more practical role for the ASW helicopter carrying Cruisers would be the hunting of NATO submarines, particularly SSBN, operating closer to the Soviet homeland, rather than providing protection for the new generation of Soviet SSBN's. The reasoning behind this role change stemmed from the reality that the new generation SSBN's would still have to operate within a few thousand kilometers of the United States coast in order for their missiles to reach their targets, particularly inland. This, it was clear, placed the helicopter carrying cruisers protecting the missile boats at particularly high risk as they would be operating in waters where NATO enjoyed an overwhelming superiority in surface and air warfare assets.

The Project 667A vessels were modified a number of times, particularly in regards to installation of new missile complexes as longer-range, and multiple warhead, variants became available in the shape of the aforementioned R-27U.

Top: The Project 667A could carry sixteen R-27 missiles arranged in two rows of eight aft of the conning tower. Above: The Project 667A missile silo compartment, with raised hatches, during assembly. PA Sevmash/Makeyev

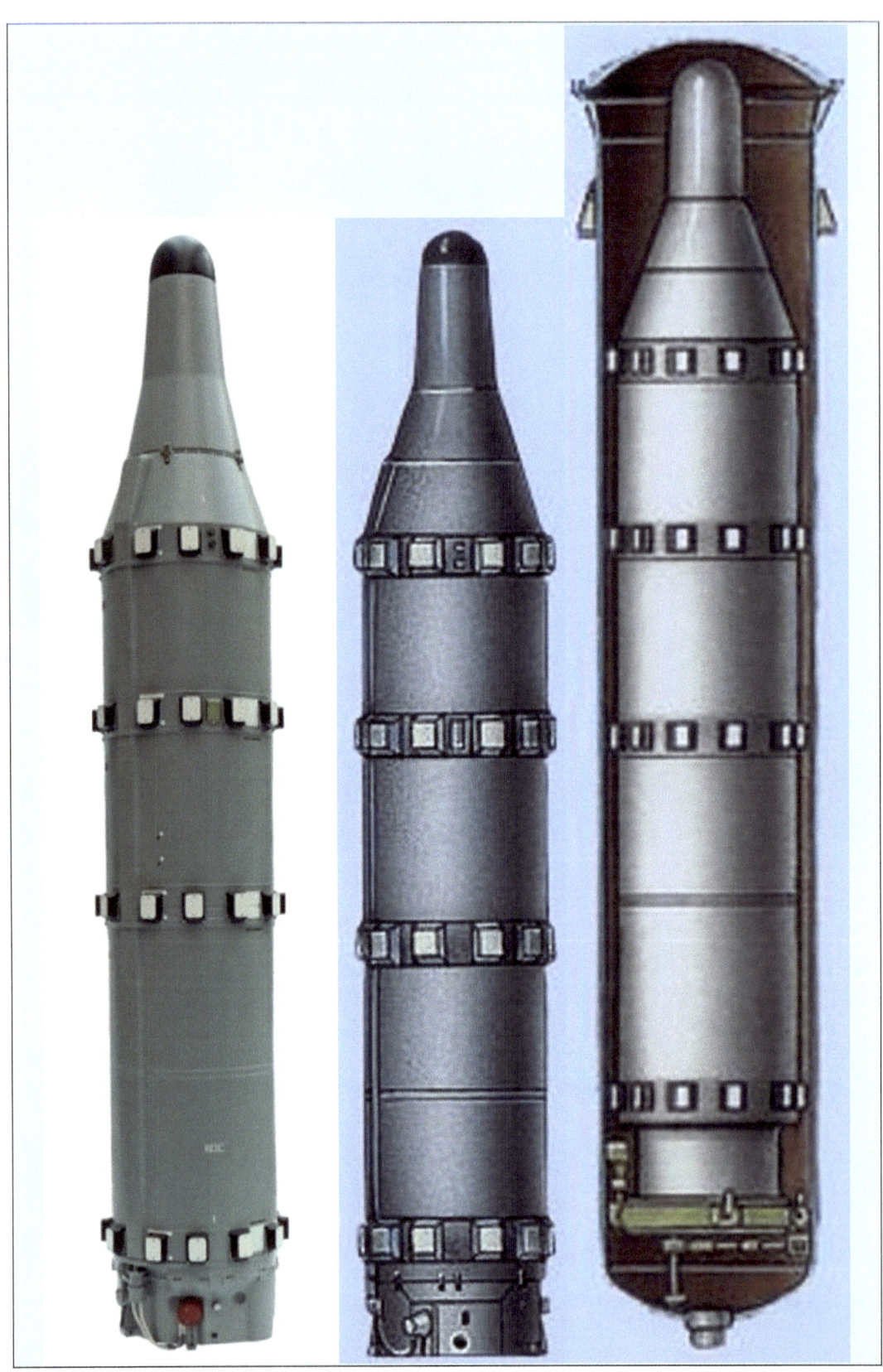

Page 42: Trio of illustrations (to slightly different scales) of the R-27 (D-5 complex), the rightmost graphic depicting the missile contained within the launch tube. Previous page: Russian language graphic showing the various compartments of the R-27 ballistic missile. Text reproduced below with English translation non-bolded in parenthesis): **боевой блок** (combat unit); **одноступенчатый носитель** (single-stage carrier); **переднее днище-приборный отсек** (front bottom instrument compartment); **амортизаторы на ракете** (shock absorbers on rocket); **бак окислителя: два полубака с переливом окислителя из нижнего в верхний** (oxidant tank: two half tanks with oxidizer overflow from the bottom in upper); **цельносварной корпус носителя; обечайки и днища вафельном конструкции** (all welded body of the carrier; shells and bottoms of waffle construction); **двухслойное межаковое днище** (double layered interatomic bottom); **бак горючего** (fuel tank); **двухблочный двигатель: центральный-замкнутый в баке горючего; рулевой-открытый, вне бака (две камеры и тна)** (a two-block engine: central-closed in a fuel tank; steering-open, outside the tank – two chambers and tones); **коническое днище, рама двигателя** (conical bottom engine frame); **переходник (в полете не участвует)** (adaptor – does not participate in flight); **газовый руль, сбрасываемый** (gas operated rudder). Makeyev

This page: A Soviet Project 667A SSBN. While this class of ballistic missile submarine could carry a powerful strike armament of sixteen R-27 ballistic missiles, the range of these weapons dictated that the submarines would operate too far forward for the Moskva Class ASW Helicopter Carrying Cruisers to be able to realistically support them in their patrol areas during hostilities, the risk to those vessels being judged too great. USN

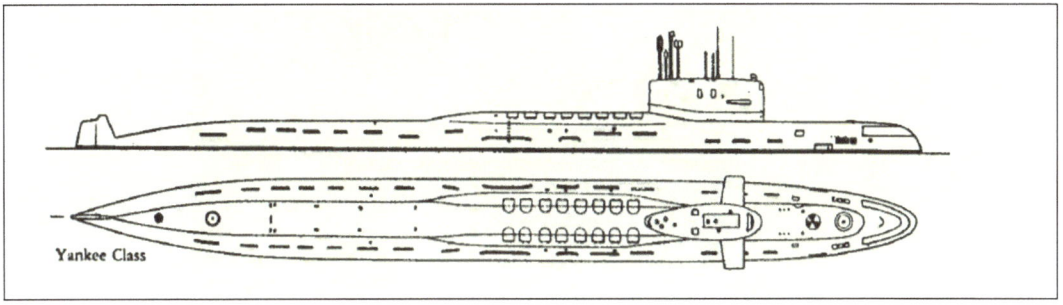

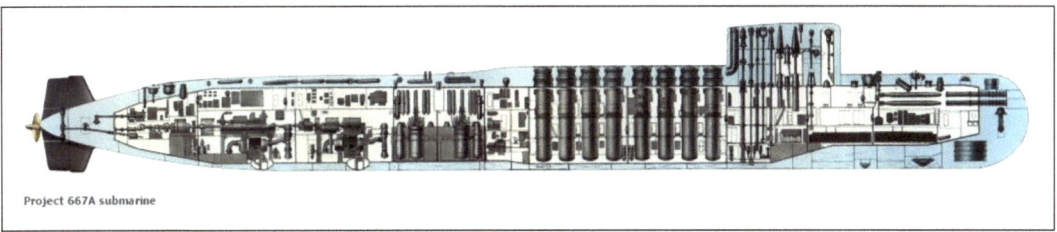

Top: Graphic from a 1984 USN intelligence assessment depicting starboard side and plan views of the Project 667A ('Yankee') class SSBN. **Centre:** Project 667A starboard side ghosted view showing the R-27 missile compartment. **Above:** Graphic depicting the launch of an R-27 missile from a Project 667 SSBN. US Gov./Makeyev/DIA

Top: The lead Project 667A boat, K-137 (later named *Leninets* (*the Flower of Lenin*)), was laid down at Severodvinsk on 4 November 1964, launched on 11 September 1966 and commissioned on 5 November 1967. While the Project 658 SSBN could dive to a depth of 320 m, the Project 677A could dive to a depth 400 m, an automatic control system preventing safe dive depth being exceeded. Above: A Project 667A ballistic missile submarine underway on the ocean surface. PA Sevmash/US DoD

Previous page: Project 667A ballistic missile submarines of the Soviet Northern Fleet. This page: A damaged Project 667A submarine observed from a NATO maritime patrol aircraft. CDB-Rubin/US DoD

Project 667A boats were introduced to the Soviet Northern Fleet, followed by the Soviet Pacific Fleet, constituting the major part of the Soviet sea-based nuclear deterrent capability by the early 1970's. NHHC

Development of the R-27 (D-5 complex), which was allocated the technological index reference 4K-10 and the NATO reporting designation SS-N-6, had commenced in 1962, the year before an operational capability was attained with the first generation R-21. The chief designer for the D-5 complex was V. P. Makeyev with Yu. K. Ivanov appointed leading designer. A new second generation SLBM program, initially identified in NATO intelligence agencies under the reporting name SARK, was displayed publicly at the November 1962 Moscow parade. The first photographic evidence showed a missile with dimensions dissimilar to then in service SLBM missiles of the R-11FM and R-13 types, leading to the conclusion that it was being developed in connection with the development of a new class of SSBN. By the late 1960's, whilst NATO still considered the SARK to be a viable SLBM program, it was further considered that no flight test had been initiated and that it may have been a mock-up for a prototype of an early design iteration for the SERB, another SLBM development conducted under the D-6 complex program (this was evaluated by western intelligence agencies as an early design integration of the missile complex that would eventually lead to the R-27) SLBM. The SERB program had been identified in western intelligence agencies when presented at a Moscow parade in November 1964. The first indication that the weapon was in flight test appeared in the form of a 1965 East European television broadcast showing the launch of what appeared to be such a missile, this being the year of the D-5 complex maiden launch.

Russian/Soviet Submarine Launched Ballistic Missiles

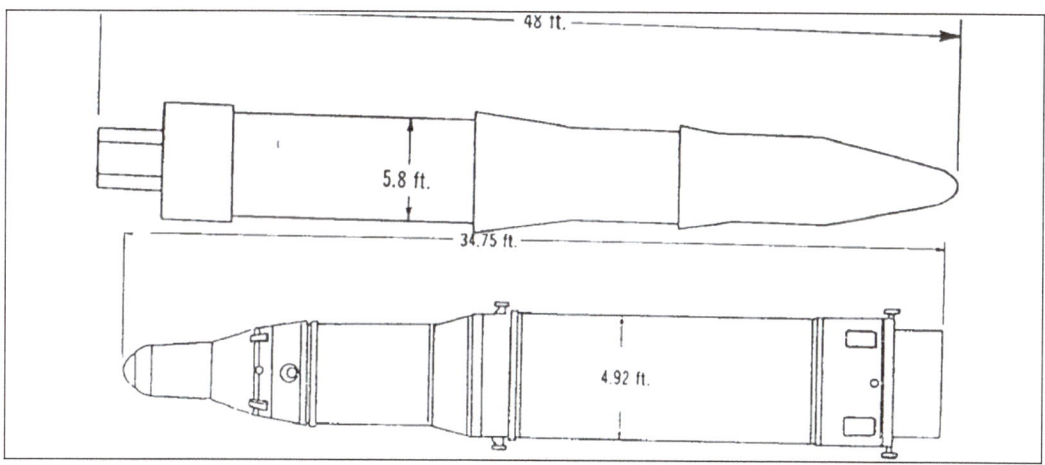

Above: Ground test/mock-up articles of the planned D-6 complex SLBM iterations. The weapon depicted in the top photograph has been referred to in intelligence documents as the SERB while the missile in the lower photograph has been referred to as the SARK. However, conflicting document evidence suggest the contrary, the missile in the upper photograph being the SARK and the missile in the lower photograph being the SERB. The planned D-6 complex lost favour to the D-5 complex (R-27 series) and was not put into service. Above: crude drawings of NATO intelligence inferences with estimated dimensions of the SARK (upper) and SERB (lower) Makeyev/ US Gov.

A Soviet Navy Project 667A submarine circa 1970's. US DoD

Length of the R-27 was reduced by around a third over that of the R-21 and launch tube volume was reduced by a factor of 2.5 resulting in an order of magnitude reduction in launch system weight – the R-27 missile itself having around a one third weight reduction over its forebear. The small dimensions of the R-27 missile and the launch tubes was enabled by adopting a number of new design approaches with not only that end in mind, but also to increase the overall capability of the missile complex and to increase the numbers of missiles carried on the submarine. Central to the reduction in overall size was the new engine arrangement, which was now housed within a fuel tank. This process required fueling and ampulization of the fuel tanks, which were welded, during the assembly process at the manufacturing plant. The design process implemented a number of other new innovations, including, as laid down in Makeyev documentation, 'wafer-type shells, rubber-metal shock absorption systems, a combination of different functions in one structural element, completely sealed bimetal un-detachable adapters…'

Firing range of the R-27, at 2500 km, was considerably in excess of that of the R-21 and accuracy was vastly improved over its forebears. By 1969, western intelligence agencies assessed the SS-N-6 (R-27) missile as having a maximum range of 1,500 nm (2778 km), slightly higher than the actual range value of 2500 km. The same intelligence assessments attributed to the weapon an accuracy in the region of 1 nm. However, while western intelligence agencies were, in 1969, providing reasonably accurate assessments of missile performance through information provided by observed parameters of test launches, those same assessments showed that the NATO intelligence community remained ignorant as to whether or not the SS-N-6 was actually deployed on the 'Yankee' class (Project 667) SSBN.

Project 667AU modification of the Project 667A armed with R-27U missile. US DoD

The Project 667A submarine was equipped with a Tucha ('Thundercloud') automatic battle management complex that collected data on environmental/weather conditions and conducted navigational calculations for use with the submarine weapons - torpedoes and ballistic missiles. The new system of automated-control for the missile pre-launch procedures reduced to ten minutes the amount of time required to bring an R-27 to readiness. One of the major capability enhancements for the Russian nuclear deterrent submarine force was the ability to salvo fire missiles at eight second intervals, all sixteen missiles able to be launched in two minutes. In comparison, the R-21 missiles arming the Project 629B and Project 658M were launched at ten minute intervals, some thirty minutes being required to launch all three missiles, leaving the submarine in a vulnerable position only 30 m or so below the ocean surface. The salvo fire capability was aptly demonstrated by the second Project 667A submarine, K-140 (this vessel was laid down on 19 September 1965, launched on 23 August 1967 and commissioned on 30 December that year), which launched eight R-27 missiles in salvo in autumn 1969.

The R-27U (retained the NATO designation SS-N-6 allocated to the R-27), development of which commenced in 1971 under chief designer V. P. Makeyev with A. P. Grebnev appointed leading designer, entered operational service in 1974. The R-27U, which constituted the missile armament for the Project 667AU SSBN (modified from Project 667A), sixteen missiles accommodate, was a development of the R-27 adapted with a three cluster low yield warhead configuration, the first Soviet SLBM so equipped. The complex could also be configured with a larger yield single warhead. Design and development of the lower yield cluster configuration warhead for the R-27U was the Soviet Union's first step towards the introduction of

MRV (Multiple Reentry Vehicle) and later MIRV (Multiple Independently (targeted) Reentry Vehicle) for its sea based ballistic missiles.

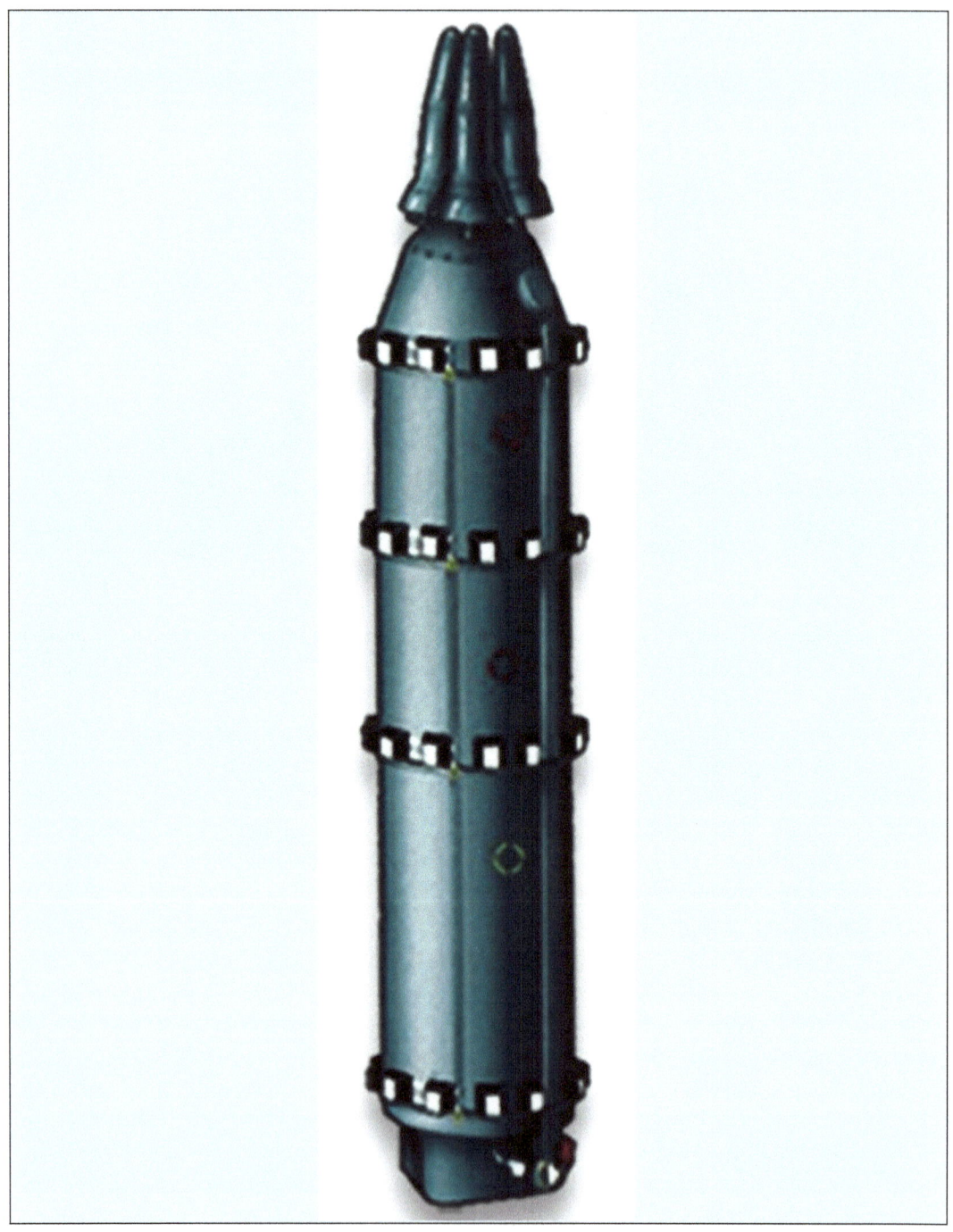

An R-27U shown in the three cluster warhead configuration. This variant could also be fitted with a single warhead of increased yield. Makeyev

**Top: R-27U warhead vehicle of the low yield three warhead cluster configuration.
Above: R-27U warhead vehicle of the higher yield single warhead configuration.**
Makeyev

When configured with the cluster unit of three warheads the R-27U had a firing range of 2500 km, the same as that of the single warhead R-27. However, when fitted with the single larger yield warhead option, firing range was increased to 3000 km, a 20% increase over that of the R-27. In addition, firing accuracy over the baseline R-27 was increased by a stated (by Makeyev) 15%, this value considered to be applicable to both single and cluster warhead configured missiles. In addition to the warhead(s) the R-27U incorporated a number of more subtle changes, including small scale improvements to the cruise engine and the on-board control system.

R-27/U (D-5 complex) – data furnished by OJSC Makeyev State Rocket Centre

Launch mass: 14.2 tons
Maximum throw weight: 1100 kg
Length: 9.06 m
Diameter: 1.5 m
Number of stages: 1
Propellant: liquid
Guidance system: inertial
Type of reentry vehicle: single reentry vehicle (R-27) and three cluster or single reentry vehicle (R-27U)
Firing range: 2500 km for the R-27 and 3000 km for the R-27U with a single warhead and 2500 km for the R-27U with a cluster of three warheads
Force of sea for missile launch: up to 5
Carrier vessel: Project 667A and Project 667AU
Number of missiles carried by submarine: 16

An R-27U ballistic missile in the three cluster warhead configuration. Makeyev

As noted above, from 1968 the R-27 would constitute the medium-range SLBM armament of the Project 667A submarines, which could carry sixteen such missiles. The rapid build-up of Soviet SSBN/SLBM force levels, combined with the equally rapid build-up of land based ICBM (Inter Continental Ballistic Missiles) and IRBM (Intermediate Range Ballistic Missiles) banging home to NATO the stark reality that the days of that alliances nuclear superiority over the Soviet Union were over and that arms control was the only logical way forward. This would, in effect, lead to the mutual acceptance of the doctrine of MAD (Mutually Assured Destruction) in that no power block had the ability to destroy the other without being destroyed itself. This reasoning would lead to the SALT (Strategic Arms Limitations Treaty) of 1972 that would limit future strategic weapons of both NATO (primarily the United States) and the Warsaw Pact (in effect the Soviet Union as no other Warsaw Pact member states possessed strategic nuclear weapons). To meet the limitations introduced by SALT the Soviet Union was faced with the need to retire a number of first generation SSB/SSBN's and re-role a handful of Project 667A SSBN's to allow for the introduction of new generation SSBN's armed with new generation SLBM. To this end, a number of Project 667A boats were retired from the strategic strike role and refitted for experimental and research work. The Project 667M conversion of 1979 was to be armed with the experimental (never deployed) 3M-25 Meteorit-M ultrasonic cruise missile (the single Project 667M (AM) conversion was delivered to the Soviet Navy in 1990 as a torpedo armed attack submarine), joining two other Project 667A's converted to 667AT attack submarine standard. Modifications for scientific and experimental work included the Project 667AK (Akson-1) and the Project 667AN, the latter being commissioned into the Soviet Navy in 1991.

Project 667A/AU missile boats served through the dissolution of the Soviet Union on 25 December 1991. The last unit, a Project 667AU, was decommissioned in January 1995, bringing to an end the operational career of the R-27/U SLBM.

Decommissioned Project 667A/AU submarine. Onega

Some Project 667A boats were converted for other roles: Project 667AT (top) and Project 667M (centre) supersonic cruise missile carrier and the design would form the basis of the Project 667B armed with the R-29 ballistic missile. CDB-Rubin

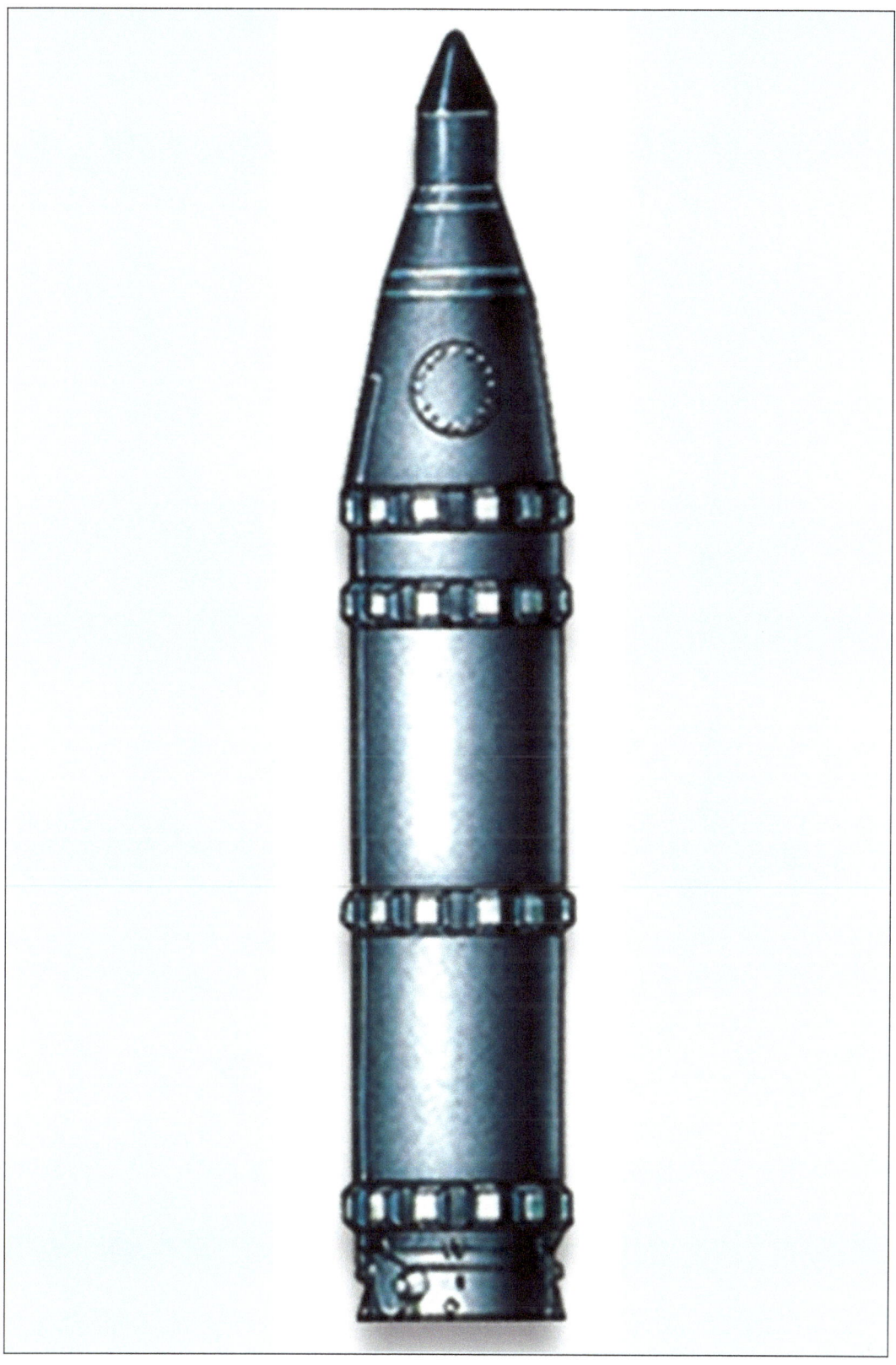

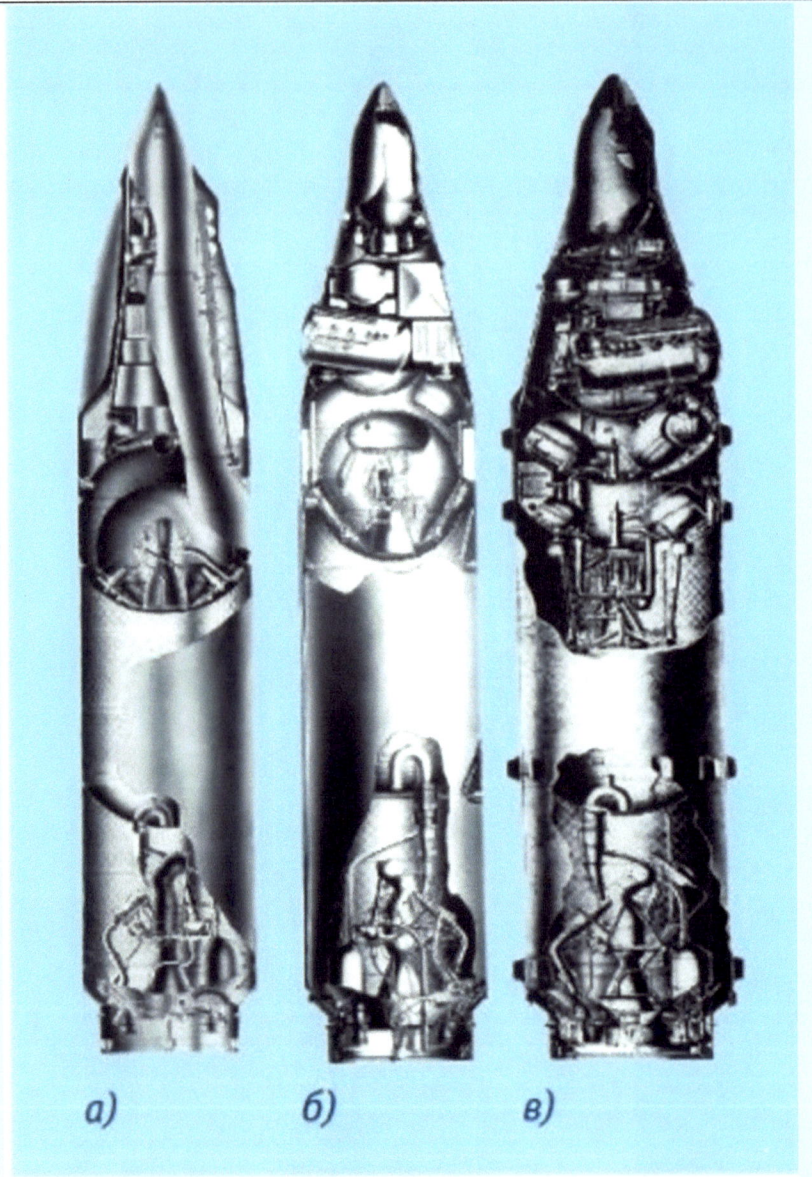

Варианты ракет Р-27К:

а) проектный – с комбинированной (баллистической и аэродинамической) коррекцией;

б) проектный – с баллистическими коррекциями;

в) реализованный – с баллистическими коррекциями.

Makeyev

An R-27K submarine launched anti-surface fleet nuclear armed ballistic missile undergoing ground tests in the 1970's. Makeyev

The R-27K (D-5 complex), development of which commenced in 1962 under chief designer Makeyev with N.D. Shepel and B. A. Seyatelev appointed leading designers, was allocated the technological index reference 4K-18, the rocket index contract PCM-25 and carried the NATO reporting designation SS-NX-6. This complex is unique among SLBM in that it was designed primarily to strike moving sea surface targets at great ranges as opposed to fixed position land targets. This anti-aircraft carrier task force development of the R-27 entered operational service testing with the Soviet Navy from 1975-1982 (the maiden launch apparently being conducted in October 1972) on modified Project 629 SSB K-102 that, post modification, carried the designation Project 605. Following a number of design iterations the Project 605 was completed with four launch tubes for the R-27K, one more that the three tube configuration of the Project 629 armed with R-11FM, R-13 or R-21 missiles.

The R-27K adopted, more or less unaltered from the baseline R-27, the first stage engine section, a number of other missile components and the missile launch system onboard the submarine. The major changes incorporated in the R-27K included the adoption of a second stage motor, the introduction of a facility for employing, as stated in Makeyev documentation, 'passive reception of radar pulses of enemy ship forces and ballistic trajectory correction with repeated ignition of the 2nd stage engine'. The design allowed for the course to be altered in extra-atmospheric flight. Thus, the second stage engine was instrumental in allowing the missile to guide itself onto a moving target such as an aircraft carrier battle group that was threatening Soviet territory. The trajectory could be corrected twice during the extra-atmospheric stage of the missiles flight. Targets would be detected through various means including relays from shadowing attack submarines, maritime patrol/surveillance aircraft (such as the Tupolev Tu-142) and orbiting satellites, such as the nuclear powered RORSAT ocean surveillance satellites.

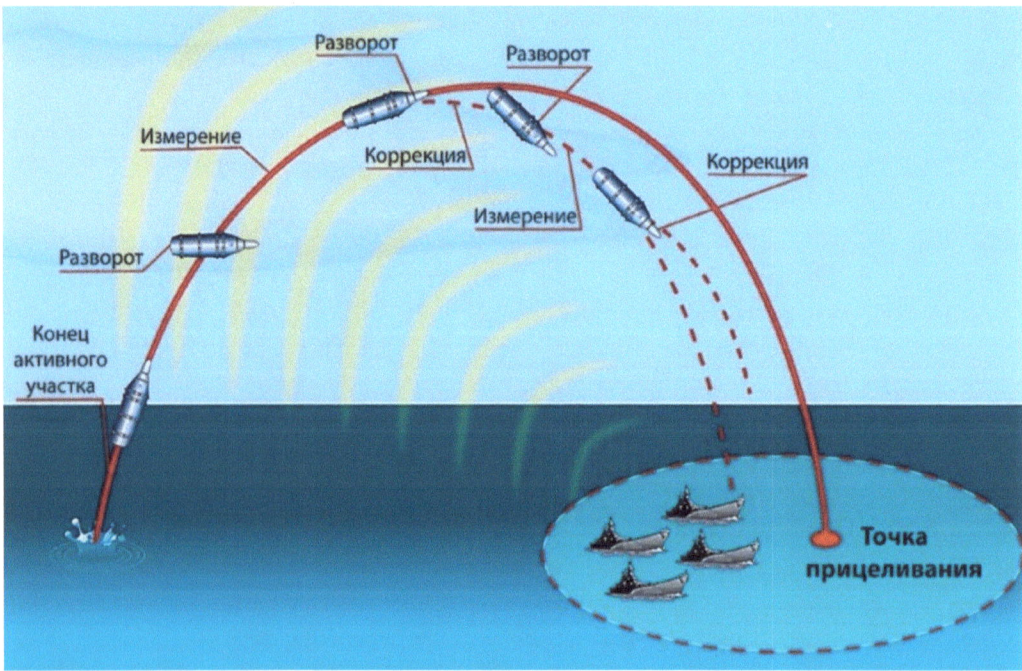

The R-27K was armed with a single nuclear warhead (top) that would home on a surface target such as an underway aircraft carrier battle group, as depicted in the Russian language diagram (above). The Russian text is reproduced below with English language translation non-bolded in parenthesis: конец активного участка (end active/effective site [missile launch]); **Разворот** (turn); **Измерение** (measurement); **Разворот** (turn); **Коррекция** (correction); **Разворот** (turn); **Измерение** (measurement); **Коррекция** (correction); **точка прицеливания** (aiming point). Makeyev

R-27K - data furnished by OJSC Makeyev State Rocket Centre

Launch mass: 13.3 tons
Maximum throw weight: 0.65 tons
Length: 9.0 m
Diameter: 1.5 m
Number of stages: 2
Propellant: liquid
Guidance: inertial and celestial
Type of reentry vehicle: single reentry vehicle
Firing range: 900 km
Force of sea: up to 5
Carrier vessel: Project 605 (modification of a Project 629 SSB)
Number of missiles carried by submarine: 4

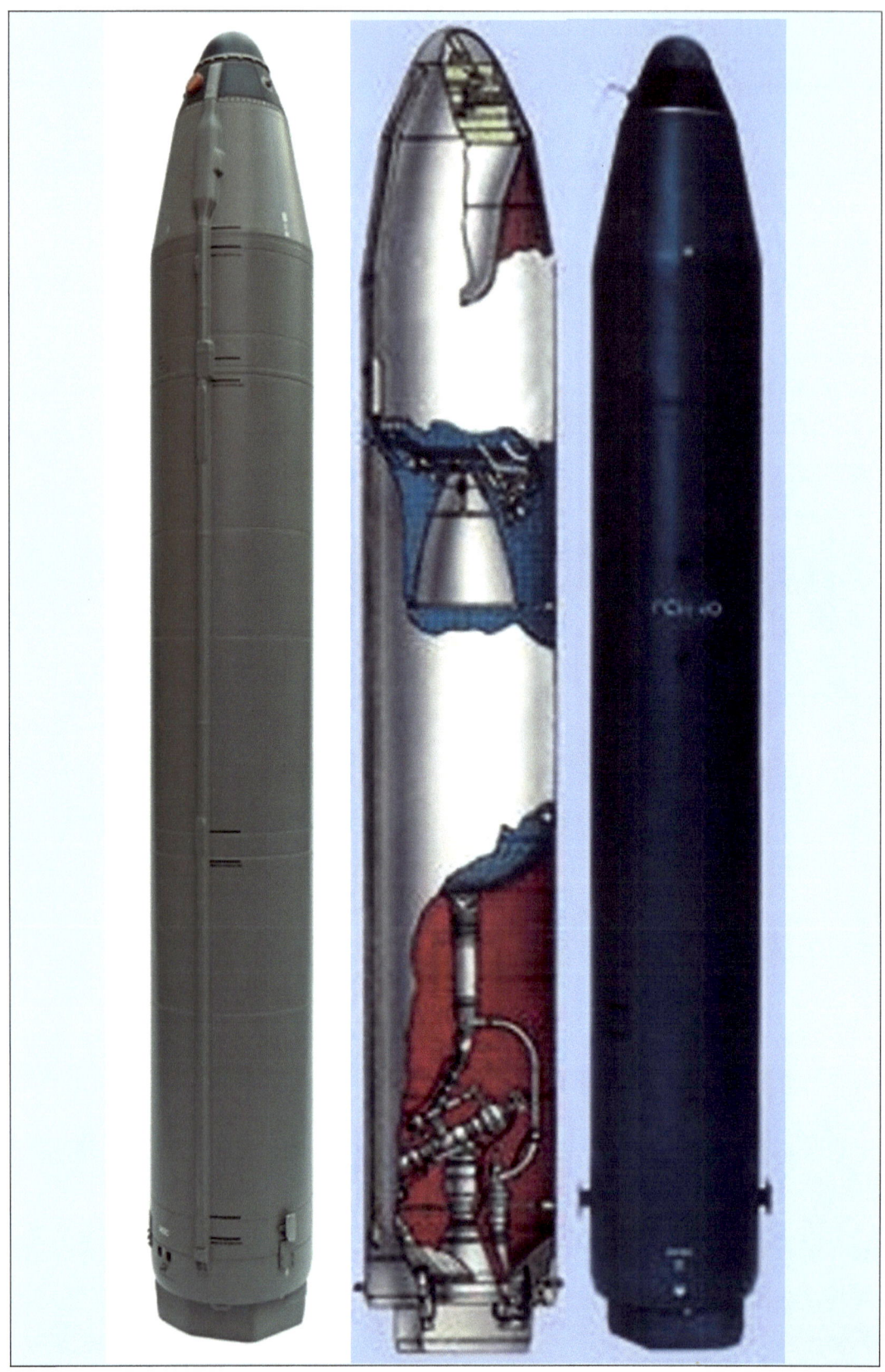

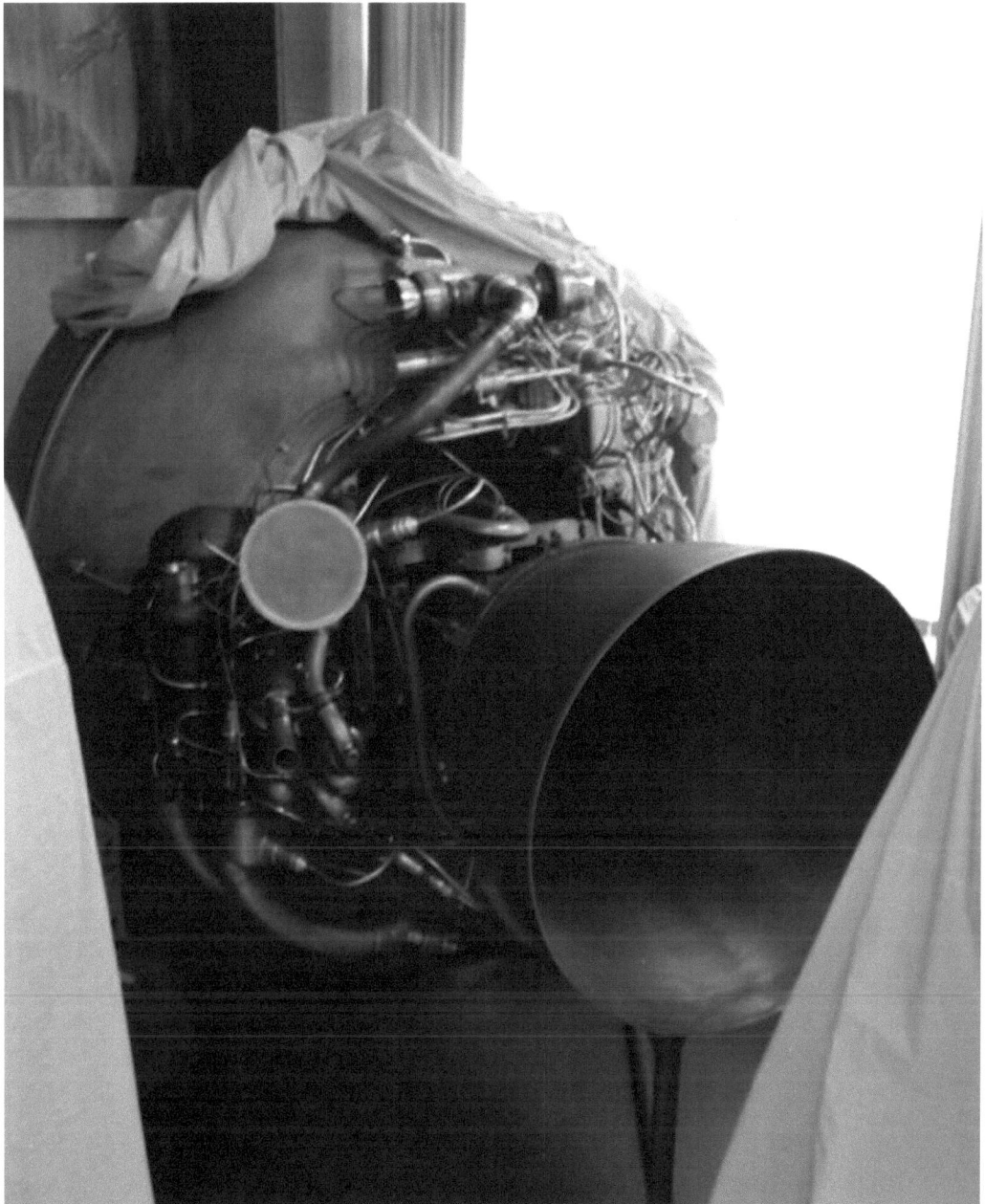

Page 62: An R-29 ballistic missile is prepared for shore based testing. Previous page: Trio of graphics, to slightly differing scales, depicting the R-29 outer configuration and, in the case of the centre graphic, a ghosted view depicting some of the interior layout. Above: A stage rocket engine exit nozzle of an R-29 ballistic missile. Makeyev

While the introduction of the Project 667A was instrumental in the Soviet Union achieving parity with NATO in SSBN strike capability, the last of the 34 boats being commissioned in 1972, it was the introduction of the Project 667B, armed with twelve R-29 (D-9 complex) SLBM's that provided the Soviet Union with a truly intercontinental strike capability for ballistic missiles launched from submarines. This enhanced strike capability reduced the vulnerability of Soviet SSBN's further as the need for such vessels to operate in waters approaching an enemy's coast was negated. The two-stage D-9 complex could deliver a single warhead to targets at true intercontinental flight range.

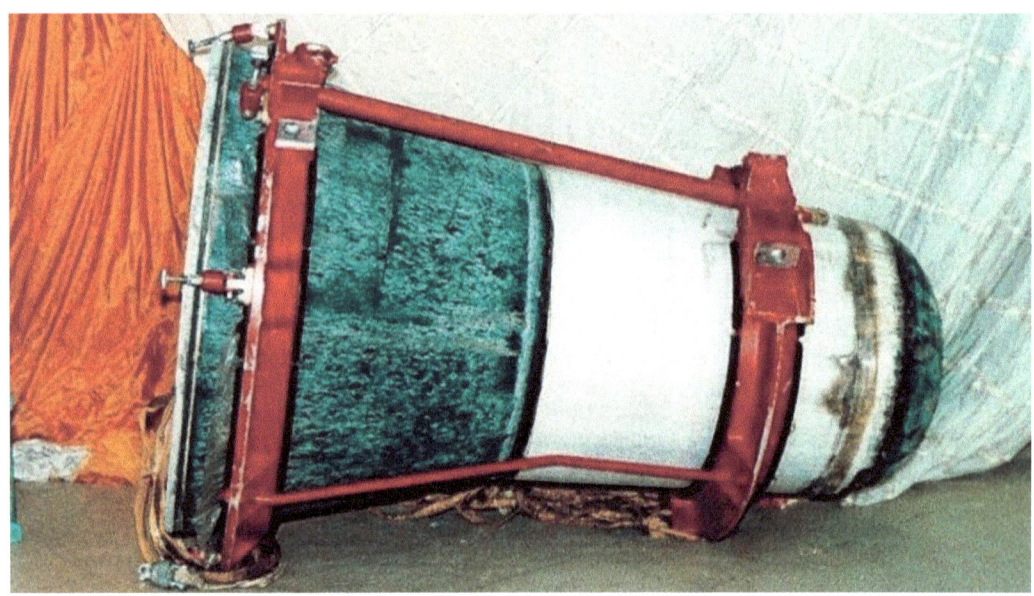

Top: The thermonuclear warhead design for the R-29 SLBM. Above: Celestial-correction complex of the type employed on the R-29. Makeyev

Development of the two-stage R-29 had commenced in 1964 under Makeyev with Yu. A. Korobeinikov appointed leading designer. The complex was allocated the technological index serial 4K-75, adopted the Soviet rocket index PCM-40 and was allocated the NATO reporting designation SS-N-8 and the NATO reporting name 'Sawfly'. The complex was first noted by NATO intelligence agencies when it was presented at the Moscow parade in November 1967. Photographic evidence indicated a two-stage missile, which, combined with its larger size in comparison to its predecessor, indicated a missile of increased range in comparison to then in-service Soviet SLBM's.

To accommodate the larger, heavier, D-9 complex, CDB-Rubin designed two new carrier/launch platforms based on the Project 667A submarine design. The first of these, the Project 667B, which was allocated the NATO reporting name 'Delta' (later 'Delta' I), could accommodate twelve missiles. The other development, designated Project 667BD (allocated the NATO reporting name 'Delta' II), could accommodate sixteen missiles. Ten Project 667B submarines were built by PA Sevmash at Severodvinsk between 1972 and 1974, a further eight being built at Komsomolsk-on-Amur. These were followed by four units of the Project 667BD. The last of these submarines was completed in 1975, the R-29 having attained an operational capability on the Project 667B the previous year.

The R-29 missile was 13 m in length, diameter was 1.8 m and starting mass was 33.2 tons. Although dimensionally larger and heavier than the R-27 series, the R-29 had a considerably improved performance over its forebears. Firing range was in the order of three times that of the R-27, bestowing upon the Soviet navy a true intercontinental range firing capability. The R-29 introduced a number of innovations, foremost among which was, as stated in Makeyev documentation, 'an all-welded body and engines submerged in the fuel and oxidizer tanks'. In its construction, the R-29, as laid down in Makeyev documentation, made 'fuller usage of the potential of shells with wafer-type rubbing'. The missile first stage contained the main stage rocket engine and the steering engines. Control was provided via gimbals mounted in two steering chambers. The second stage propulsion unit, accommodated in the oxidizer tank of the missile stage, was of the nature of a gimballed single-chamber engine. The separation of the stages was accomplished by a series of pyrotechnics, stated in Makeyev documentation as 'an extended circular explosive charge due to the pressurized gases energy' that severed the rigid structures securing the two stages of the missile.

As well as inertial navigation, the R-29 introduced a system for celestial trajectory adjustment, an innovative astro-correction complex that provided course corrections through positional fixes from observations of the Sun and distant stars. This bestowed upon the complex high accuracy when employed against intercontinental range targets, even if significant errors had been made during input of navigational data in regards to heading. The astro-correction system and other instrumentation was housed in the missile nose in order to facilitate the requirement for star sighting during measurement taking. The warhead section was housed behind the nose instrumentation compartment, both able to be removed and replaced without the missile having to be removed from the carrier submarine launch tube.

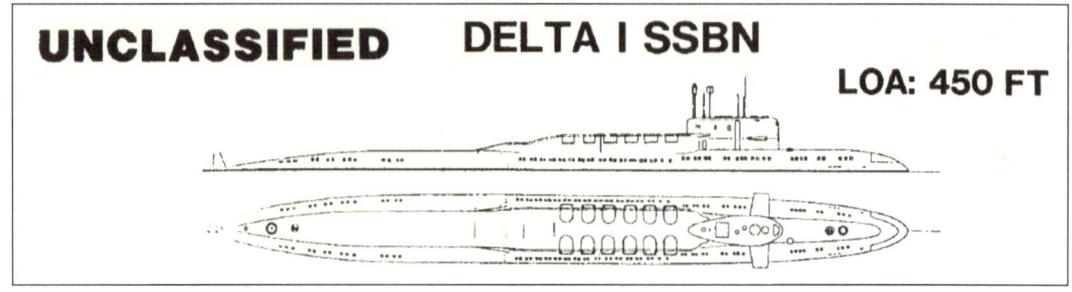

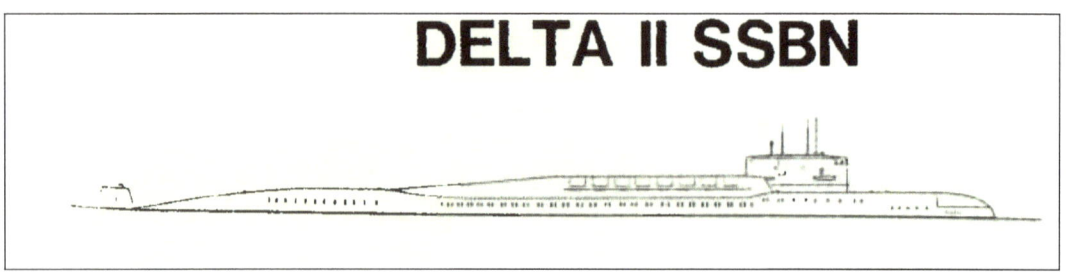

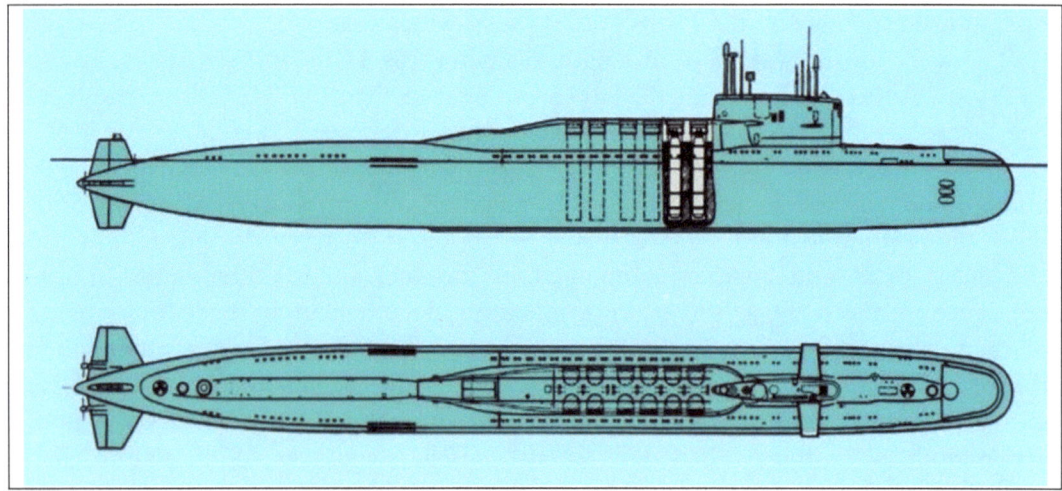

Top: Starboard side profile and plan view of a NATO intelligence drawing of the Project 667B ('Delta' I) strategic missile carrier showing only an approximate value for length. Centre: Starboard side on view of a NATO intelligence assessment drawing of the Project 667BD ('Delta' II). Above: Starboard side profile and plan view of the Project 667B strategic missile carrier. *Makeyev*

To aid penetration of potential missile defences the R-29 was equipped with a suite of penetration aids (decoys), the first Soviet SLBM so equipped. The R-29 also possessed increased throw-weight compared to its forebears and could operate in severe weather conditions in autonomous mode, which included the ability of the carrier submarine to ripple fire missiles whilst submerged, a capability first introduced with the Project 667A/R-27.

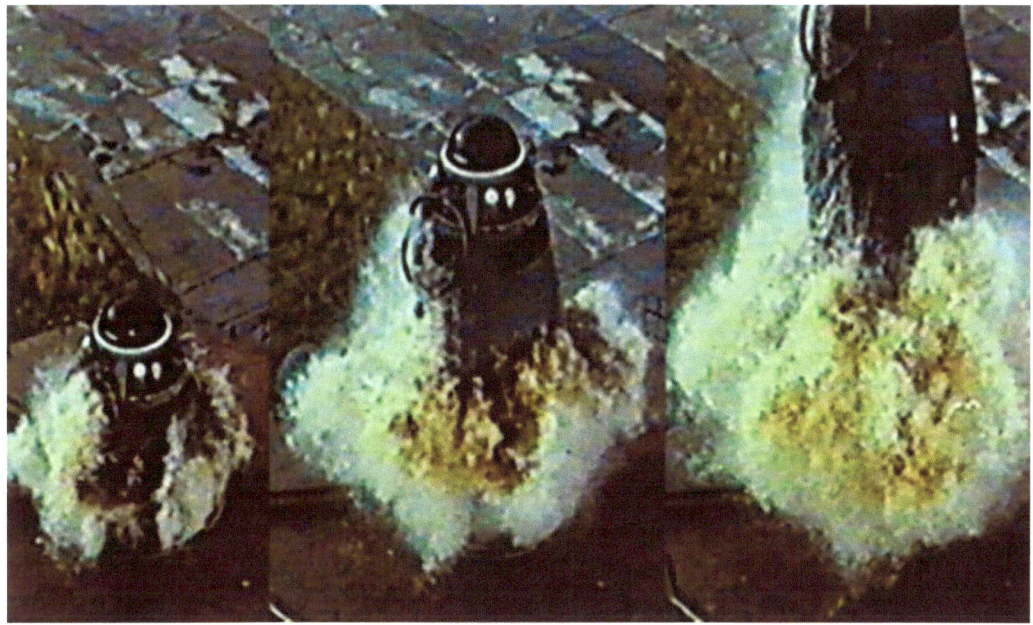

Three still footage of an R-29 test launch. Makeyev

As well as the incorporation of the onboard computer system as an integral element of the missile control system, the D-9 complex introduced a new design of submarine pre-launch and launch control centred on a main computer complex. This would facilitate a reduction in the time required for the pre-launch procedures through the integration of the computer systems of the missile and the submarine missile control system. These systems were instrumental in easing the ability to salvo launch the missiles, either submerged or surfaced, from the submarine, which adopted a launch system that incorporated reusable rubber-metallic shock absorbers mounted on the walls of the missile launch tubes.

Submerged launches could be conducted whilst the submarine was underway and at sea states up to 8, providing the facility to launch in extremely adverse weather conditions. As would become a major element of Soviet SSBN doctrine, the R-29 missile launch submarine would be allocated a mission profile that called for missiles to be launched from the submarine base by a submarine on alert. The missiles were also optimised for launch from far northern latitudes in the high Arctic Circle, which decreased vulnerability of the submarine carrier, particularly when operating under the ice pack. The principle of operating under the Arctic ice lay in surfacing through areas of polynya (areas of open liquid ocean water where sea ice would have been expected to form). If no natural polynya could be found then the submarine could surface by forcing its way up through areas of thin ice, following which it would be prepared to launch its missiles.

The Soviet Union's capability for submarine patrolling under the Arctic ice pack, surface and missile launch, was aptly demonstrated on 3 July 1981 when a Project 667B submarine surfaced through the ice and salvo launched a number of R-29 missiles. This test mission was the culmination of several years of planning and development testing of various systems to provide for a high degree of confidence of operating under such adverse conditions. The results would be carried over to the third generation Soviet submarine launched ballistic missiles that were then under development.

> R-29 (D-9 complex) – data furnished by OJSC Makeyev State Rocket Centre
>
> **Launch mass:** 33.3 tons
> **Maximum throw weight:** 1.1 tons
> **Length:** 13.0 m
> **Diameter:** 1.8 m
> **Number of stages:** 2
> **Fuel:** liquid
> **Control system:** astro-inertial
> **Type of reentry vehicle:** single reentry vehicle
> **Firing range:** intercontinental
> **Force of sea:** all-weather (up to 8)
> **Carrier vessel:** Project 667B and Project 667BD
> **Number of missiles carried by submarine:** 12 (Project 667B) and 16 (Project 667BD)

Previous page: An R-29 ballistic missile is launched from a Project 677B submarine at a high Arctic latitude on 3 July 1981. This was the culmination of several years of operational planning/testing to introduce a capability for operations under the sea ice at high Arctic latitudes. This page: The Project 667B submarine having surfaced through the Arctic sea ice on 3 July 1981. Makeyev

The R-29 constituted the ballistic missile armament of the Project 667BD. Makeyev/NHHC

The two-stage R-29D, development of which commenced in 1976 under Makeyev with N.F. Cherepov appointed leading designer, entered operational service in 1978. This was basically an R-29 modified by the removal of the penetration aids that in the R-29 were housed in the second stage tank. The warhead, which remained the same as that of the R-29, could be delivered 1200 km farther than that of the R-29. The R-29DU designation was allocated to R-29D missiles equipped with a new warhead, this variant attaining an operational capability on Project 667BD submarines in 1986.

4

THIRD GENERATION SOVIET/RUSSIAN SUBMARINE LAUNCHED BALLISTIC MISSILES

With the implementation of the R-27 and R-29 missile programs the Soviet Union had, from the late 1960's through the late 1970's, vastly increased the overall capability of that nations submarine based element of her nuclear deterrent triad. Not least among the capability enhancements had been the introduction of an intercontinental range strike capability courtesy of the R-29. From the late 1970's, the Soviet Union continued to increase the capability of her SLBM (Submarine Launched Ballistic Missile) force in the face of United States force modernisation through the retirement of older Polaris systems and the introduction of Poseidon and later Trident C3 missile systems. In regard to the Soviet SLBM force modernization this resulted in the introduction of several new missile complexes and submarine project launch platforms on which the missiles would be deployed.

The first of what would be termed third generation SLBM complexes was the R-29R (D-9R complex), sixteen of which were carried by Project 667BDR Strategic Missile Cruisers from 1974. The R-29R introduced a MIRV (Multiple Independent Reentry Vehicle) warhead capability whilst retaining the option for single warhead delivery to targets at true intercontinental flight range. No official values for range have been released, but based on development and operational testing, unofficial estimates, although varied, are typically in excess of 9000 km. This not only allowed the new generation Soviet SSBN's to operate in protected waters closer to the Soviet homeland where the Project 1123 ASW (Anti-Submarine Warfare helicopter carrying Cruisers and Project 1143 HACC (Heavy Aircraft Carrying Cruisers) could provide support, but also facilitated the ability to strike a wider diversity of target sets from the submarine home base, without the need to go to sea.

The introduction of the R-39 (D-19 complex) on the Project 941 SSBN, twenty missiles carried, each with up to ten MIRV, occurred in 1983. The R-39 featured extended intercontinental flight range allowing Project 1143 and Project 1123 vessels deployed to Northern or Pacific Fleet regions to operate in better protected waters under cover of Soviet land based aircraft.

The R-29R (D-9R complex) introduced a MIRV warhead capability to the Soviet submarine launched ballistic missile fleet. Makeyev

The two-stage R-29R (D-9R complex), development of which had commenced in 1973 under chief designer V. P. Makeyev with A. L. Zaitsev appointed leading designer, entered operational service in 1977. This missile complex was allocated Soviet the technological index serial 3M-40, the Soviet rocket index PCM-50 and the NATO reporting designation SS-N-18.

The R-29R retained the same body configuration, with the engines encapsulated within the fuel and oxidizer tanks, which was a major design feature of the R-29. Fueling with the liquid fuel and encapsulation of the tanks was conducted during the manufacturing process at Krasnoyarsk Machine-Building Plant (factory) (JSC KRASMASH). As with the R-29, the first stage contained the main rocket engine and the steering engines, gimbals mounted in the two steering chambers providing control. The second stage engine, which, as was the case with the R-29, was accommodated in the oxidizer tank of the missile stage, adopted the gimballed single-chamber engine as was the case with its forebear. Control in the pitch and yaw planes was provided by, as laid down in Makeyev documentation, 'swinging the engine in a corresponding plane', whereas roll control was accomplished by redistribution of the pump turbine exhaust gases through the roll control nozzles.

Makeyev documentation states that the 'engine section of the upper stage included four-chamber liquid-fuel engine, propellant tanks and a case and provides for individual targeting of each reentry vehicle within a large-radius zone. On the outside surface of the case, engine combustion chambers and nozzles are mounted and inside there are propellant tanks shaped as toroid parts. The engine automatic control elements and the steering actuator are arranged in the central part of the section. The engine has an open-loop configuration with a turbine-pump fuel supply system. Pitch and roll control is provided by redistribution of thrusts of the pairs of chambers placed in corresponding stabilization planes'.

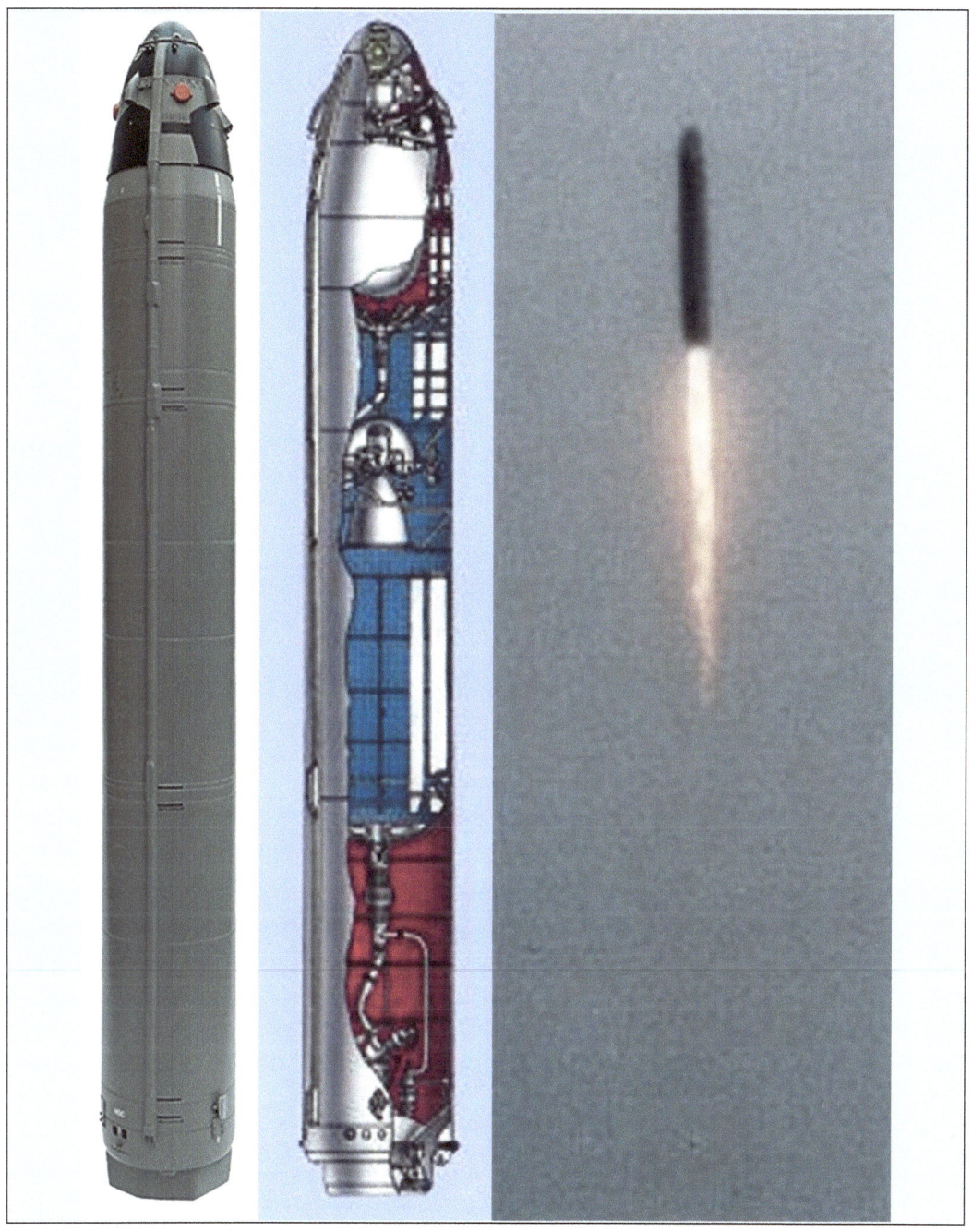

Two graphics of the R-29R SLBM and a photograph of such a missile being launched from a Project 667BDR submarine The graphic at left depicts the outer lines of the R-29R and the partially ghosted view graphic at centre shows some internal compartments of the various missile stages. Makeyev

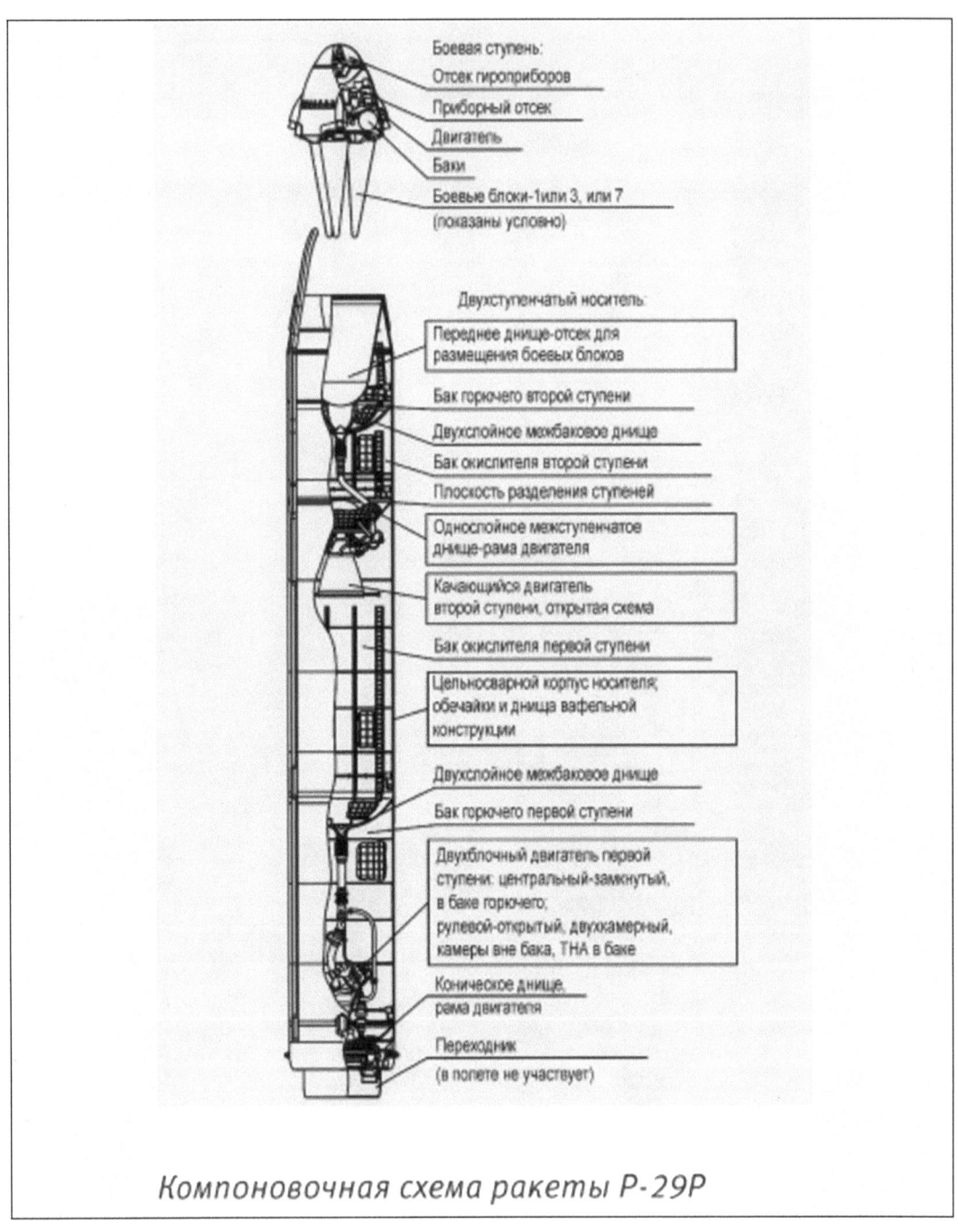

Russian language diagram of the R-29R two-stage submarine launched ballistic missile. The diagram shows the main missile stages and the combat stage (can accommodate a single MIRVed warhead (not detailed in the graphic) or combinations of three or seven MIRVed thermonuclear warheads), the instrument compartment, stage fuel and oxidizer tanks and stage engine compartments. Makeyev

R-29RL submarine launched ballistic missiles during the manufacturing process. Makeyev

Both stages were the same diameter and were separated in the same process as that employed for the R-29 missile. The upper stage contained the stage engine, warhead section and a sealed instrumentation compartment. The latter, located in the nose of the missile, housed the autonomous inertial control system and the astro-correction flight-trajectory complex, the astro-dome itself being jettisoned during the missile flight. The instrument compartment, however, should be considered as two separate compartments divided by a sealed bottom. One of these compartments contained a three-axis gyro-stabiliser with an integral astro-sighting system/astro-correction system, this bestowing a significant increase in accuracy over that of second generation missiles. As laid down in Makeyev documentation, 'The control system equipment is mounted on a frame without individual shock absorbers for its elements and the frame is attached to the instrument section ring with shock absorbers'.

The R-29R complex introduced a three middle class yield warhead MIRV capability and a new warhead arrangement. The new small-size warhead design embodied a high-speed reentry vehicle, which had a low dispersion when in the post-reentry trans-atmospheric phase of the flight. The missile was designed with three warhead configurations – single, three MIRV and seven MIRV. Under the terms of START-1 (Strategic Arms Reduction Treaty-1) R-29R missiles were deployed with the three MIRV head. The warhead section, which is located in an area determined by Makeyev as the 'concave upper bottom' of the fuel tank that feeds the second stage engine, contained the warhead reentry vehicles and associated equipment, such as the frame and cables for the reentry vehicle fixing (in-place) and vehicle release. The reentry vehicles, which were securely mounted on a frame, would be released at the appropriate point of the missile flight and separated by the onboard control system, allowing the warheads to be independently targeted at different aim points.

For the most part the R-29R retained the same ground support and maintenance procedures as the R-29, this also being the case for the submarine based launch system. The R-29R was carried on Project 667BDR (NATO reporting name 'Delta' III) SSBN's, fourteen such vessels being built between 1976 and 1982, the first of which joined the Soviet navy in 1976.

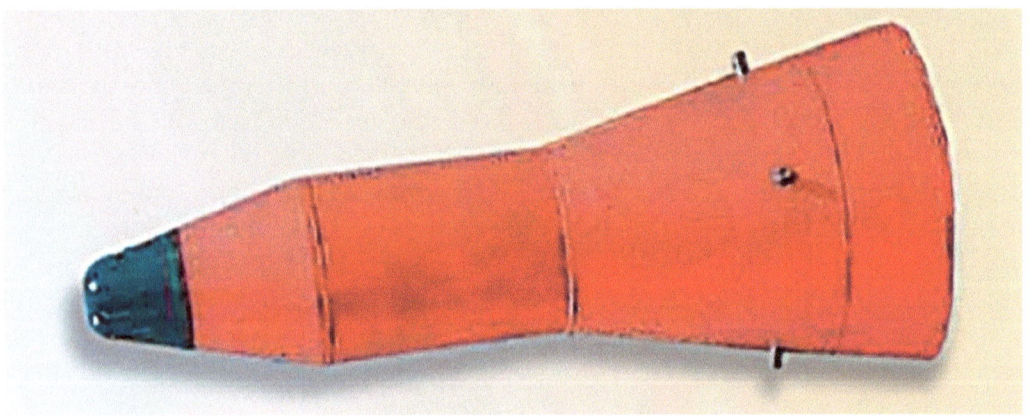

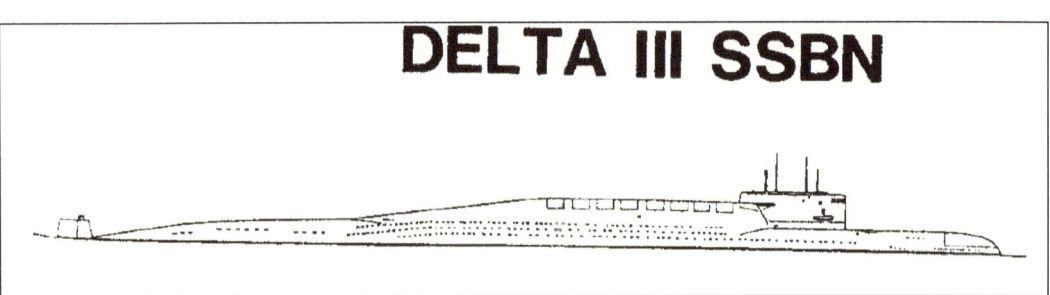

The R-29R medium yield warhead vehicle (top) and low yield warhead vehicle (centre). To carry the R-29R CDB-Rubin designed the Project 667BDR strategic missile carrying submarine (above). Makeyev/US Gov.

An R-29R missile is hoisted to or from a land based test silo, representative of a Project 667BDR launch tube, during development testing. Makeyev

R-29R/RKU2 (D-9R complex) – data furnished by OJSC Makeyev State Rocket Centre

Launch mass: 35.5 tons
Maximum throw weight: 1.65 tons
Length: 14.1 m
Diameter: 1.8 m
Number of stages: 2
Fuel: liquid
Control system: astro-inertial
Type of reentry vehicle: single reentry vehicle and MIRV capability of 3 medium yield or 7 low yield warheads
Firing range: intercontinental
Force of sea for missile launch: all-weather
Carrier vessel: Project 667BDR
Number of missiles carried by submarine: 16

Among the capability enhancements introduced with the extended R-29R family was progressive improvement of the ability to conduct operations in high Arctic region areas of polynya (open liquid ocean water where sea ice would be expected to form) in the Arctic Ocean. Launches from these high latitudes, previously conducted with R-29 missiles from a Project 667B submarine, not only provided safety from enemy countermeasures for the launch submarines, but also reduced missile flight time over the pole to its target in the Continental United States, thereby reducing reaction time for defensive countermeasures. US DoD

Top: An R-29RL missile is lowered into a test silo on a shore based test rig of a Project 667BDR submarine launch tube. Above: An R-29RL is launched from a berth side submarine platform demonstrating the complex's operational launch from base capability. Such vessels would be on alert when not at sea. Makeyev

Graphic depicting an R-29RL ballistic missile being launched from a high Arctic latitude after the submarine has surfaced through a suitable area of polynya or thin ice. Makeyev

Previous page and above: R-29RK. The photograph at the top of page 83 is also stated to be an R-29RM in some Makeyev documentation, it certainly being more akin to an R-29RM in regards to its external features. Makeyev

There were no less than four further developments of the R-29R complex that would be covered under the third generation of Soviet SLBM's. All of these derivatives retained the two-stage configuration of the R-29R. The first such development to be fielded was the R-29RL (D-9RL complex), development of which commenced in 1975 under Makeyev with A. L. Zaitsev appointed leading designer. This complex, which entered operational service in 1979, was fitted with a new warhead section able to accommodate seven high-speed reentry vehicles with a new medium yield warhead designed under authorization of decrees of the Soviet government issued in August 1975 and June 1976 respectively. Range was increased by around 8-9% when a single high yield warhead or a three smaller yield warhead cluster was employed. The R-29RL could be operated aboard Project 667BDR submarines alongside the R-29R, courtesy of the Atoll ship-board digital computer system, which was optimised for the simultaneous operation of both missile variants.

R-29RKU submarine launched ballistic missile. Makeyev

An R-29RKU-01 being loaded aboard a Project 667BDR submarine test complex.
Makeyev

The R-29RL was followed by a further development designated R-29RK (D-9RK complex), which achieved an operational capability with the Soviet Navy aboard a Project 667BDR submarine in 1982. This variant, development of which had commenced in 1980, was designed under chief designer Makeyev with A. L. Zaitsev appointed leading designer. The major design change was the incorporation of a new warhead section able to accommodate either a three MIRV or a seven MIRV cluster of high speed, small size, but increased yield (over previous small warheads) warheads. Further improvements were made to missile accuracy, this being stated by Makeyev as being in the order of 40% over that of the R-29 second generation missile.

A further modification of the R-29RK resulted in the R-29RKU, development of which commenced in 1985 under general designer I. I. Velichko with A. L. Zaitsev appointed leading designer. This variant, which achieved an operational capability with the Russian Navy on a Project 667BDR submarine in 1987, introduced a new low yield warhead design and an increase of the capability of the missile to be successfully launched when the carrier submarine was operating at high Arctic latitudes through a tried and tested navigation complex. Other modifications included implementation of an adaptive modular structure. For operation from the Project 667BDR submarines, such vessels had installed a new digital computer system and modifications were made to the shore-based maintenance and service infrastructure and equipment, allowing the R-29RKU and unmodified R-29R missiles to be put in operation alongside each other on the Project 667BDR submarines of the Pacific Fleet.

An evolution of the R-29RKU resulted in the R-29RKU-01 (D-9RKU-01 complex), development of which commenced in 1986 under general designer I. I. Velichko with A. L. Zaitsev appointed leading designer. This missile complex, which achieved an operational capability on a Project 667BDR submarine in 1990, was developed in response to Soviet government decrees issued in February 1985 and October 1986. The first called for the enhanced ability to be fired from high Arctic latitudes while the second called for the introduction of a new middle-yield class warhead design to replace the warheads designed for the R-29R, R-29RL and R-29RK missile complexes. The warhead design for the R-29RM was selected of the R-29RKU-01, this adopting an advanced development of carbon composite material. Developmental flight tests of the warhead were conducted under what is simply stated in Makeyev documentation as 'different entry conditions'.

The R-29RKU-01 added to the missile types that could be operated on the Project 667BDR submarine alongside each other in asymmetric combinations of variants.

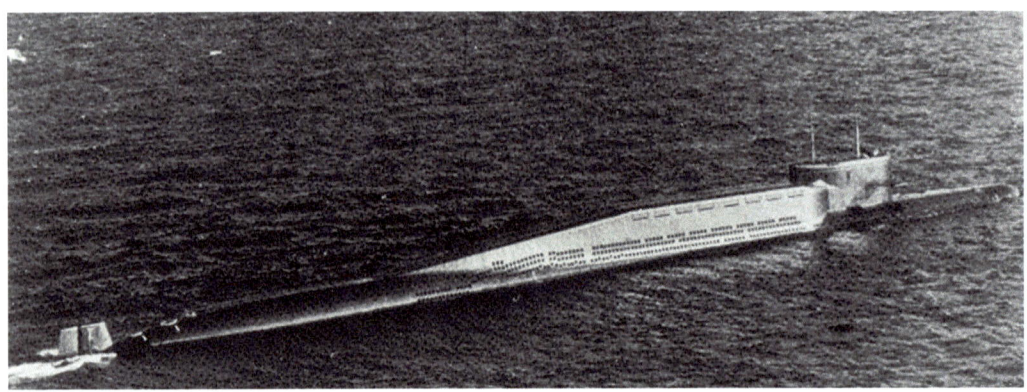

Top: Basic starboard side outline of the Project 667BDR SSBN from a 1984 US intelligence document. Centre and above: Project 667BDR SSBN's. US Gov

Project 667BDR SSBN's. US DoD/Makeyev

Previous page: Graphic depicting a ghosted view (left side of graphic) of the R-31 (D-11 complex) submarine launched ballistic missile detailing the staging engines, solid propellant tanks and the reentry vehicle section for the single nuclear (thermonuclear) warhead. The right side of the graphic depicts the R-31 housed in a missile launch tube designed for the Project 667AM ballistic missile submarine, a conversion from a Project 667A. Above: Graphic depicting the R-31 (D-11 complex) submarine launched ballistic missile on a stand in the assembly shop. KB Arsenal

While it would have been a fair assessment to state that Makeyev was the major player in Soviet submarine launched ballistic missile design, other design bureaus continued to develop such weapon systems. The R-31 (D-11) complex, which was designed and developed by KB Arsenal, was the first Soviet solid-propellant ballistic missile designed to be deployed aboard a submarine, Soviet submarine launched ballistic missile design taking major step forward.

Designed by Tyurin Peter Alexandrovich (chief designer of ballistic missiles at KB Arsenal from 1971-1981), the R-31 (allocated the NATO reporting designation SS-N-27) was deployed aboard the single Project 667AM SSBN - twelve missiles carried. The primary function of the Project 667AM submarine, which was a conversion from a Project 667A boat, was the development and operational testing of the D-11 missile complex. The vessel conducted harbor and shipyard sea trials before embarking upon state acceptance testing, joint flight testing of the D-11 missile complex commencing in 1976. The Project 667AM submarine constituted an element of the Soviet Navy SSBN force armed with the R-31 complex from 1980 until 1990 when it was withdrawn from operational service as a ballistic missile submarine.

R-31 basic technical and operational characteristics – data furnished by KB Arsenal

Operational range: ~4000 km
Head part (warhead section): monoblock nuclear with the capability for cluster warheads
Starting mass: ~27 tons
Length: 11 m
Maximum body diameter: 1.54 m
Deployment vehicle [platform]: Project 667AM
Number of missile carried on Project 667AM: 12
Launch parameters: can be launched sub-surface whilst the submarine is cruising courtesy of the pressure accumulator
Firing time to launch all missile: 55 seconds (12 missiles launched ~4.6 second intervals
Storage period on board submarine: 10 years

Only a single Project 667AM (above) was converted from a Project 667A submarine, apparently K-140. Post modification this vessel could carry and launch the R-31 (D-11 complex). The R-31 itself was not adopted for widespread service with the Soviet ballistic missile submarine fleet, which, in a similar timeframe was adopting a number of designs including the R-39 that would be operated from the Project 941 Heavy Underwater Missile Cruisers. CDB-Rubin

The R-39 (D-19, complex), development of which commenced in 1973 under general designer V. P. Makeyev with A. P. Grebnev appointed chief designer and V. D. Kalabukhov appointed leading designer, entered operational service with the Soviet Navy in 1983. The D-19 complex was allocated the technological index serial 3M-65, the Soviet rocket index PCM-52 and was allocated the NATO reporting designation index SS-N-20.

Project 941 Akula class submarine of the Taifun (Typhoon) Strategic Sea-based System armed with R-39 ballistic missiles. CDB-Rubin

The three-stage R-39, the first Soviet SLBM to be powered by a two-chamber solid-propellant fuel propulsion system, incorporated a SMLS (Shock-mounted Missile Launch System). This was a launch pad bearing, mounted in the upper section of the missile launch tube on the Project 941 submarine, which enabled the missile to remain suspended when placed in the tube. With the missile in the launch tube the SMLS, as laid down in Makeyev documentation, 'damps the missile, seals the launch tube and ensures missile safety in the submarine, allowing dipping [diving] of the submarine to great depth with the open launch tube cover'. Other than the missile support belt, all of the load-bearing parts of the missile required for land and submarine based operations are incorporated within the SMLS and the missile tail section, these being jettisoned post-launch in the initial flight phase - a few seconds after the missile breaks the surface of the water and transitions to airborne flight.

The launch phase, necessitated by the requirement to force the missile out of the tube and free of the water, is a complicated affair, described in Makeyev documentation as follows: 'The missile is ejected from a "dry" launch tube by the cartridge pressure accumulator placed on the launch tube bottom in the 1st stage engine nozzle. At missile lift-off the special solid propellant charges located on the SMLS provide for protection in the form of a gas-jet cavern that considerably reduces the hydrodynamic loads acting on the missile. The command to start the 1st stage engine is generated at the instant the missile leaves the launch tube. If the 1st stage engine fails to start up, the missile, after its appearance on the water surface, is moved away from the submarine for safety purposes. The launch system is separated from the missile in flight by special engines and is also moved way'.

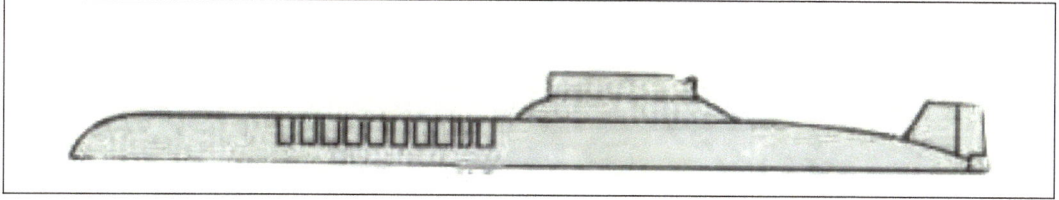

Top: Port side view drawing of a Project 941 (NATO reporting name 'Typhoon') class submarine taken from a 1980's USN intelligence assessment. Centre: US intelligence agency graphic depicting the submerged launch of an R-39 (SS-N-20) ballistic missile from a Typhoon class submarine. Above: Graphic depicting the replenishment of missiles on a Typhoon class SSBN. US Gov./DIA

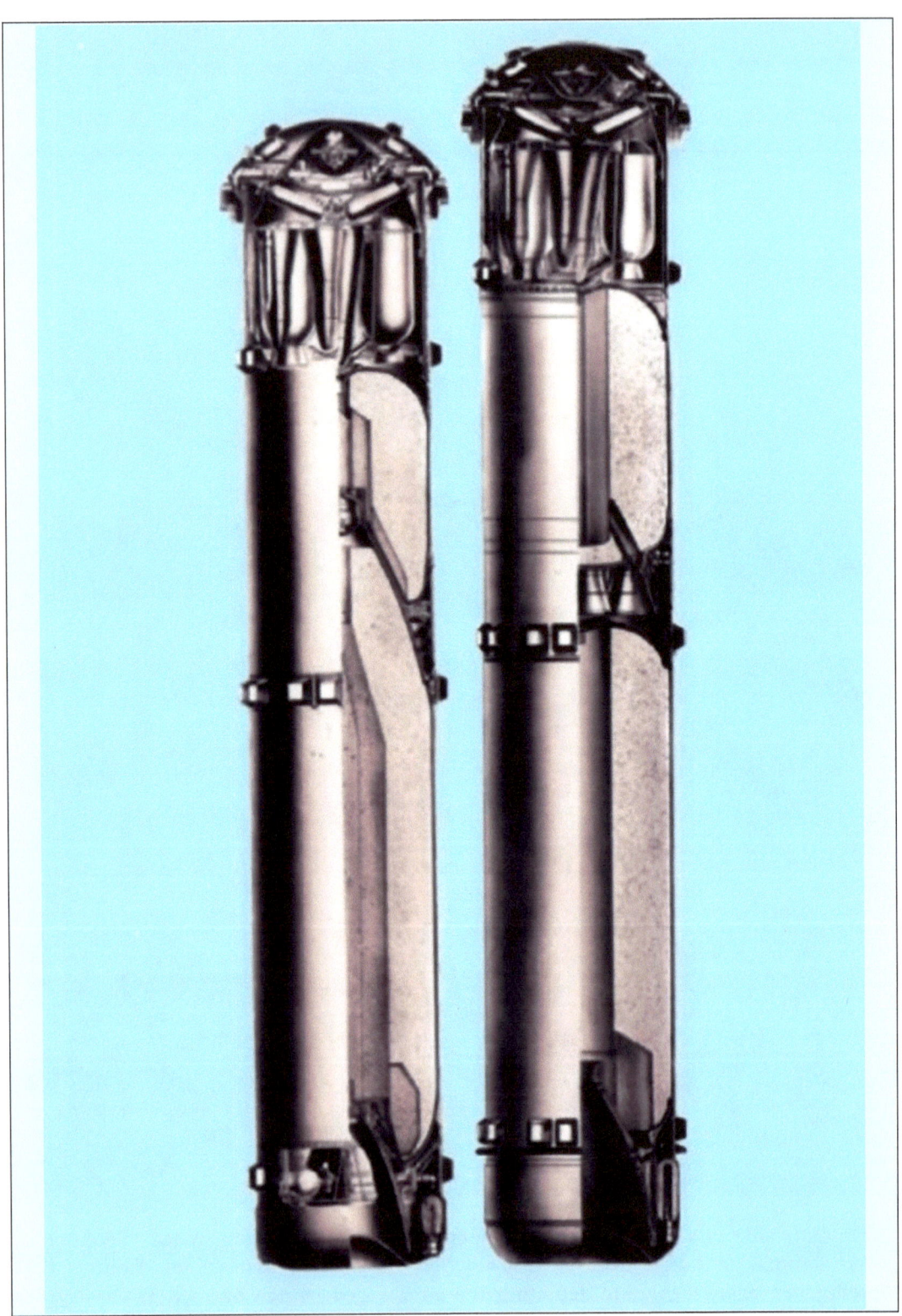

Previous page: Graphic depicting a draft iteration of the proposed R-39 at (right) and the final R-39 design (left). Above: Graphic depicting the outer lines of the R-39 missile. Makeyev

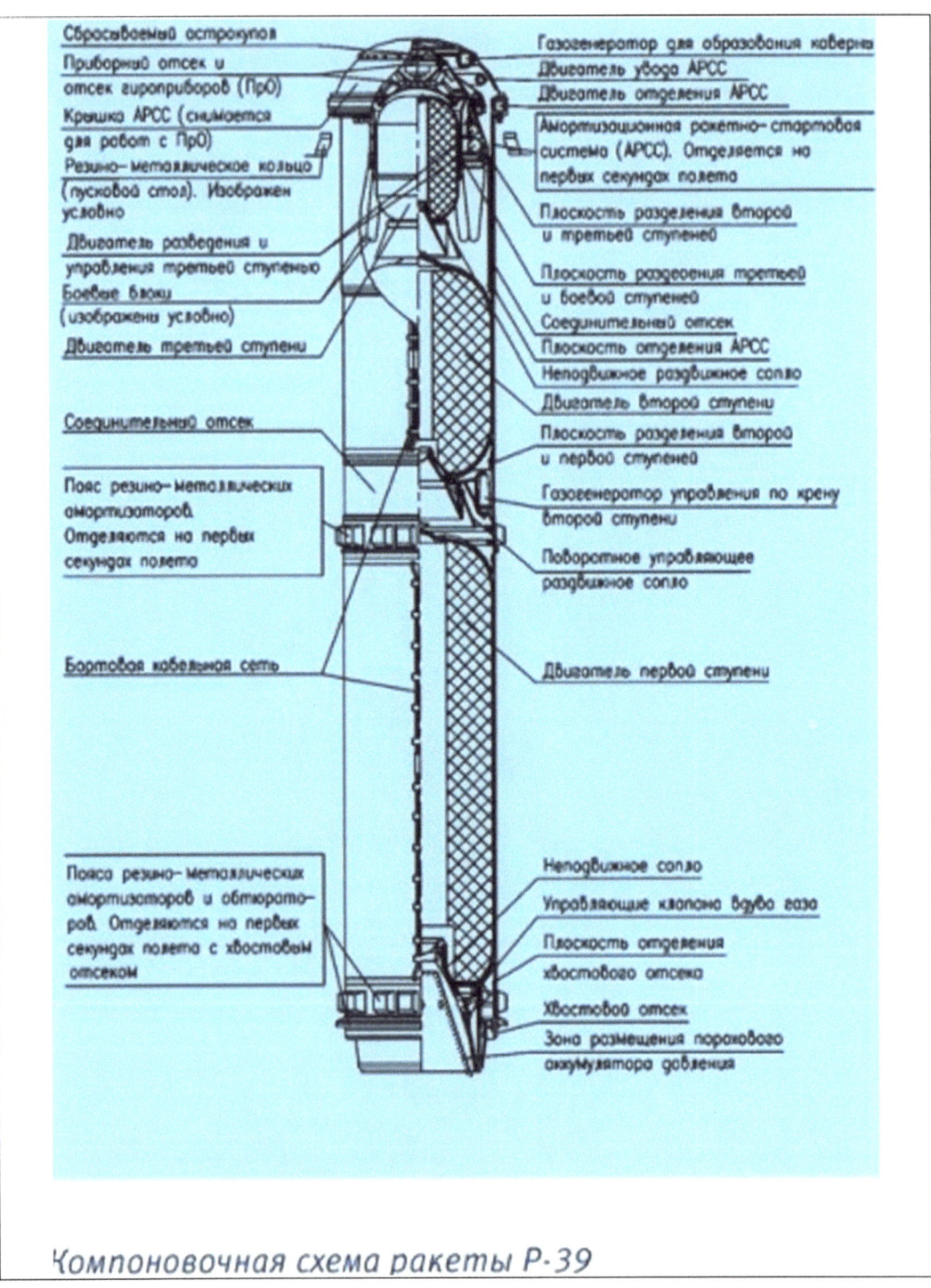

Russian language diagram of the R-39 ballistic missile that depicts major areas of significance including the three main stage sections, stage engines, stage propulsion tanks, MIRVed warhead section and the instrumentation section. Makeyev

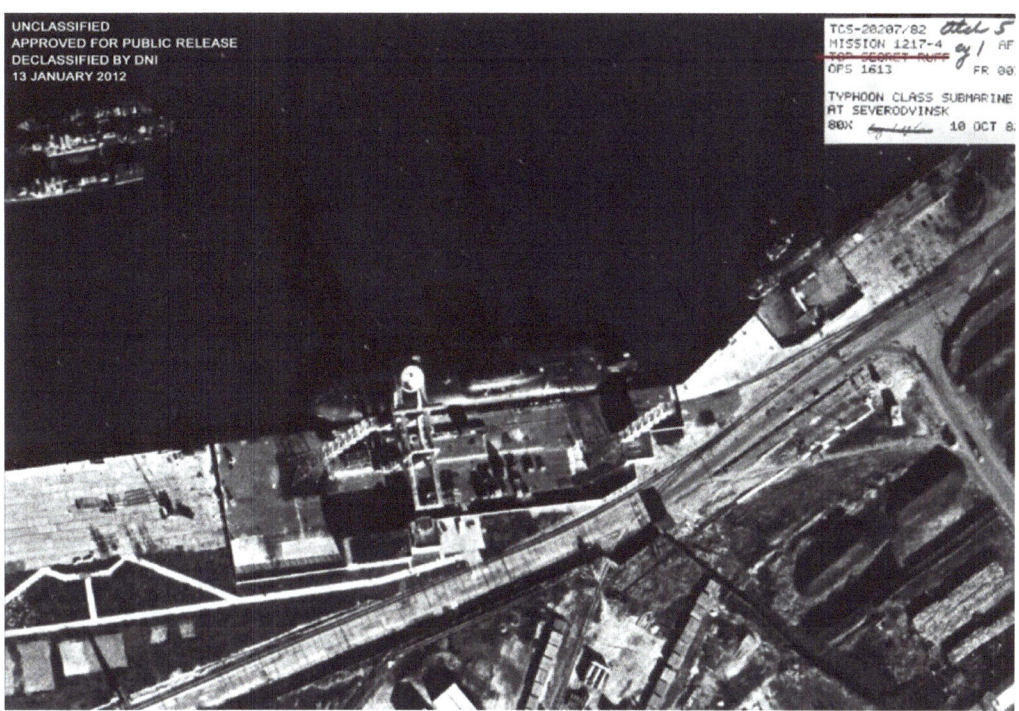

Top: This photograph (declassified and released in 2012), taken on satellite mission 2017-4, of a Project 941 'Typhoon' class submarine at Severodvinsk on 10 October 1982 left NATO analysts in no doubt as to the colossal size of the new Soviet ballistic missile submarine by comparison to the Destroyer/Frigate size warships in the upper left of the photograph. Above: A graphic released by the MODRF depicting the sole operational Project 941U, *Dmitry Donskoy*, at the 2017 Naval Parade. US Gov./MODRF

An R-39/U launched from a submerged Project 941/U Heavy Ballistic Missile Submarine. Makeyev

An R-39/U ballistic missile of the D-19/U complex. Makeyev

As laid down in Makeyev documentation, 'despite a shock-absorbing missile launch system available in the front part, which replaced the launcher and ensured the missile protection at off-nominal submerging of a submarine, the missile structure allowed replacement of reentry vehicles and the equipment bay without unloading the missile from a silo [submarine launch tube]. The missile and complex breakthrough technologies were implemented in structural, thermal-protective and erosion-resistant materials'.

Previous page and above: Project 941 Akula (Typhoon) class submarine of the Strategic Sea-based System of the Soviet Navy circa mid to late 1980's. US DoD

The R-39's Yuzhnoye designed 3D65 second stage steering motor, rated at 205.8 kg vacuum thrust, burned a high-energy T-98K-8E solid-propellant mixture, producing a vacuum specific impulse kgf²/kg of 274, with a SRM loaded mass of 52.65 kg. The upper section of the missile would house the instrument section and what was termed the dispensing stage, the latter containing the warhead MIRV's, both sections being joined by a flange. A new generation of high velocity reentry vehicles of small size was developed for the R-39, these carrying warheads of increased specific power in comparison to small warheads previously deployed on Soviet SLBM. The ten MIRV reentry vehicle warhead section, which was located around the rear part of the third stage engine, included the MIRV's, a compartment for control equipment and a liquid-fuel rocket engine that allowed each of the MIRV's to be independently targeted. The shock-mounted launch complex housed the missile for extended periods of standing during transit and when housed in the submarine missile silo (launch tube).

The instrument section, located in the upper most part, the missile nose, actually formed two separate sealed compartments, which, by design, were divided by an intermediate panel. Instrumentation included a free gyro and an astro-sighting/correction system covered by a protective dome on the ground or in the submarine launch tube. This dome was jettisoned once the missile transitioned to flight. A control system was also located in the instrument compartment, this, as laid down in Makeyev documentation, being 'arranged on a shock-mounted frame'.

The conning tower of the Project 941 submarine was designed and built on a massive-scale, even for a vessel as large in overall dimensions and mass as the Akula class Heavy Ballistic Missile Cruisers of Taifun (Typhoon) Strategic Sea-based System. MODRF/US DoD

Five of the six Project 941 SSBN's completed are shown at the Soviet Northern Fleet base at Polyarny, Northern Russia, in the late 1980's. CDB-Rubin

The dispensing stage, containing the reentry vehicles carrying the warheads, was located below the instrumentation compartment to which it was joined by the aforementioned flange. The dispensing stage included a dual-mode liquid-propellant propulsion unit for warhead dispensing and the third stage rocket engine.

To carry the new generation of SLBM that emerged as the D-19 complex, CDB-Rubin designed the colossal Project 941 Akula class Heavy Ballistic Missile Cruiser (also referred to as Heavy Nuclear Underwater Cruiser or Heavy Missile Nuclear Submarine Cruiser), the largest submarine design ever built. The new submarine class was designed under chief designer S. N. Kovalev with an emphasis on providing, as stated by Rubin, 'an innovative aggregate-and-modular method of construction', which took place at Severodvinsk (PA Sevmash). This facility had undergone large-scale reorganisation, available facilities being more or less doubled, in the mid-1970's as it prepared to undertake construction of the third generation strategic missile carrying nuclear submarines. The first of the Project 941 submarines, TK-208, had been built by 1981 and was commissioned that same year. Six Project 941 submarines were built by PA Sevmash at Severodvinsk from 1981 to 1989.

The Project 941 introduced remote automated control of the main control and much of the other submarine systems. Living conditions for the crew was vastly improved over previous generation designs and the number of ballistic missiles that could be carried, twenty R-39, was in excess of the sixteen R-29/R carried by its predecessor, the Project 667BDR, despite the R-39's considerably increased mass compared with its forebears. Although the US Ohio class SSBN could carry 24 Trident SLBM, the throw weight of the smaller American missile was dwarfed by the 2250 kg throw weight of the R-39, resulting in Trident being encumbered with considerably less flight range as well as being armed with smaller warheads of considerably lower yield in comparison to its Soviet generational counterpart.

The conning tower on the Project 941 was located further aft than on the Project 667 series, this facilitating the installation of twenty missile silos forward. Makeyev

The D-19 complex was a colossal leap forward in submarine launched ballistic missile capability, there being no western counterpart that could equal it for range and throw weight. Together with the Project 941 Heavy Ballistic Missile Cruiser (Submarine) and a newly developed port-based support system centred on a railway car complex, the D-19 complex constituted what would become the Taifun (Typhoon) Strategic Sea-based System that remains in service with the Russian Federation Navy in 2018.

R-39 (D-19 complex) – data furnished by OJSC Makeyev State Rocket Centre

Launch mass: 90 tons
Maximum throw weight: 2.55 tons
Length: 16 m
Diameter: 2.4 m (first and second stages)
Number of stages: 3
Fuel: solid
Control system: astro-inertial
Type of reentry vehicle: Ten MIRVed warheads
Firing range: intercontinental
Force of sea: all-weather
Carrier vessel: Project 941
Number of ballistic missiles carried by submarine: 20

Project 941 Heavy Ballistic Missile Submarine – data furnished by the MODRF

Displacement: 23200 tons on the sea surface and 48000 tons submerged
Powerplant: 2 x nuclear reactors delivering 190 MW; 20 steam turbine delivering 50000 bhp.
Operational diving depth: 450 m
Maximum speed, freeboard: 12 knots
Maximum speed, Mob one: 25 knots
Crew: 160
Endurance: 120 days
Ballistic missile armament: 20 x R-39 (D-19 complex - RSM-52) ballistic missiles and 20 torpedoes of mixed types - ASW, anti-surface vessel

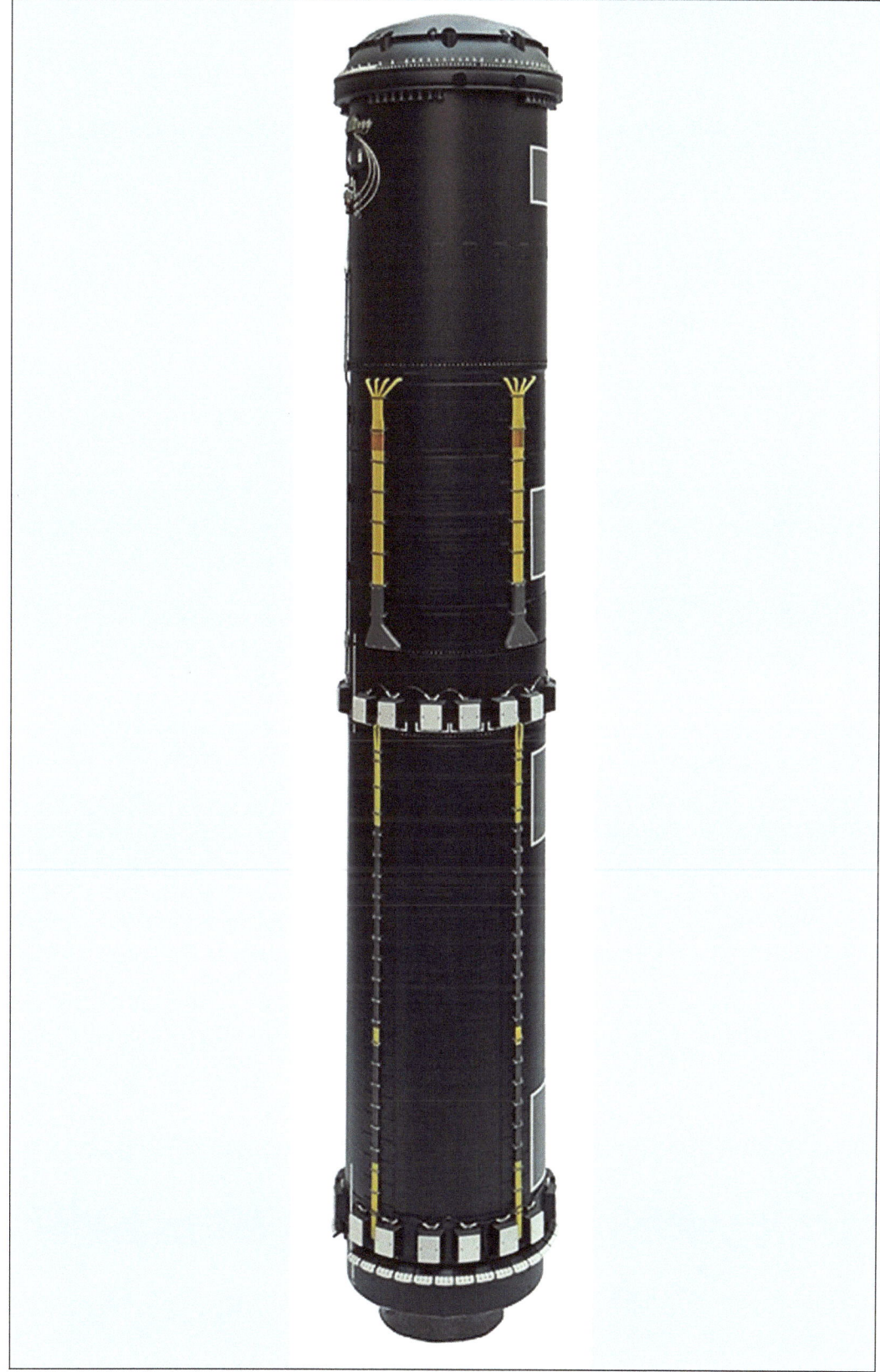

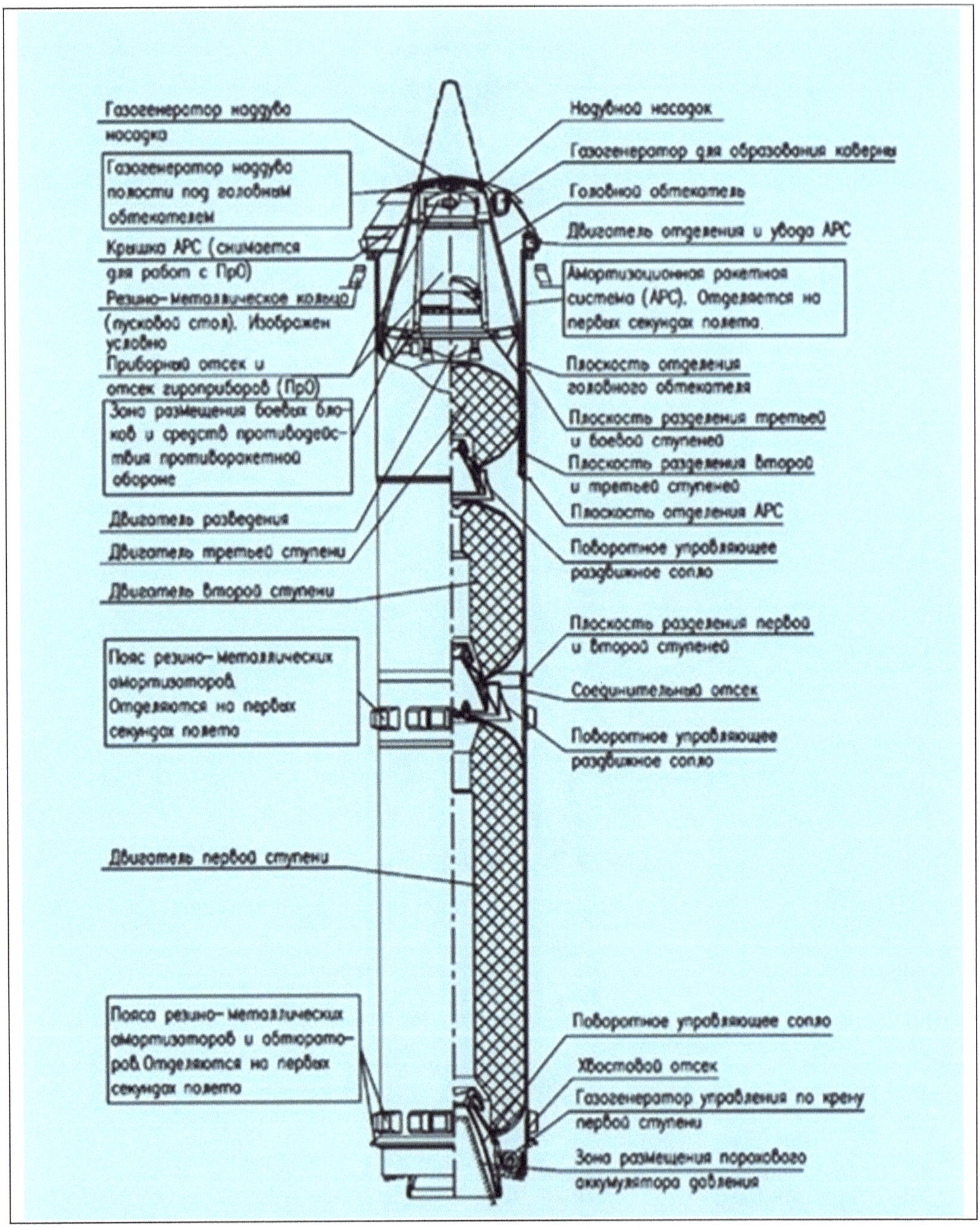
Газогенератор наддува насадка
Газогенератор наддува полости под головным обтекателем
Крышка АРС (снимается для работ с ПрО)
Резино-металлическое кольцо (пускового стола). Изображен условно
Приборный отсек и отсек гироприборов (ПрО)
Зона размещения боевых блоков и средств противодействия противоракетной обороне
Двигатель разведения
Двигатель третьей ступени
Двигатель второй ступени
Пояс резино-металлических амортизаторов. Отделяются на первых секундах полета
Двигатель первой ступени
Пояса резино-металлических амортизаторов и обтюраторов. Отделяются на первых секундах полета
Надувной насадок
Газогенератор для образования каверны
Головной обтекатель
Двигатель отделения и увода АРС
Амортизационная ракетная система (АРС). Отделяется на первых секундах полета.
Плоскость отделения головного обтекателя
Плоскость разделения третьей и боевой ступеней
Плоскость разделения второй и третьей ступеней
Плоскость отделения АРС
Поворотное управляющее раздвижное сопло
Плоскость разделения первой и второй ступеней
Соединительный отсек
Поворотное управляющее раздвижное сопло
Поворотное управляющее сопло
Хвостовой отсек
Газогенератор управления по крену первой ступени
Зона размещения порохового аккумулятора давления

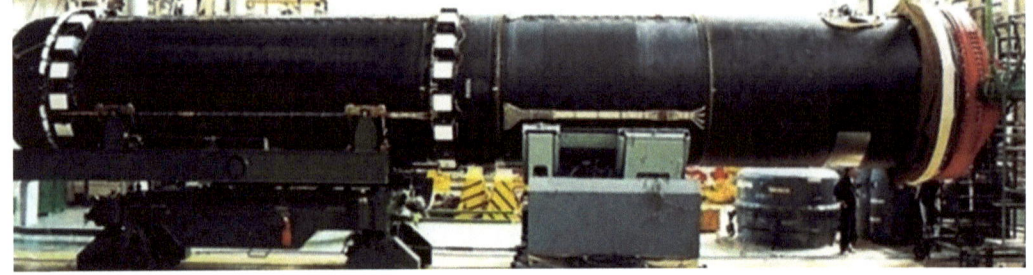

Page 107: Graphic depicting the outer lines of the R-39UTTKh (UTTH) submarine launched ballistic missile. Previous page top: Russian language diagram of the R-39UTTKh ballistic missile that depicts various areas of significance, including the three main stage sections, stage engines, stage propulsion tanks, warhead section and the instrumentation section. Previous page bottom: An R-39 development article during shore based tests. Above: Project 941/U submarine *Dmitry Donskoy*. Makeyev

Two further major developments of the R-39 were undertaken, the first being the R-39U, design of which commenced in 1985 under general designer I. I. Velichko with A. P. Grebnev appointed leading designer. This variant entered service on a Project 941U (modified 941) submarine in 1988. The major change with the R-39U was the introduction of the low-yield warhead that had been designed for the R-29RMU, the missiles being tried and tested in high Arctic latitudes. The Project 941 submarines so armed were modified to Project 941U standard, incorporating subtle changes to accommodate the operation of the R-39U.

In 1986, two years prior to the operational debut of the R-39U, development commenced of the R-39UTTKh (UTTH) 'Bark', which was designed under general designer I. I. Velichko with V. L. Kalabukhov appointed chief designer and A. P. Grebnev appointed leading designer. This missile complex, development of which ended in 1998, did not enter operational service. It was intended to retain the R-39 basic missile and launch tube dimensions and the launch procedure more or less unchanged. As with the R-39U, a move was made to a medium yield warheads and accuracy against maximum range targets was to be increased by a factor of four. Survivability was to be enhanced by a factor of 3-4 against the effects of a nuclear blast and new generation penetration aids were to be incorporated to overcome potential missile defence developments. The capability enhancements included the ability to launch the missile along what Makeyev documentation states as 'maneuvering trajectories (flat, high angle, with random drifts in arbitrary planes etc.) with the deployment of warheads with an arbitrary and enlarged zone'. Such trajectories would have further complicated missile defense counter actions.

By the time the development test program to prove the cruise and auxiliary engines for the R-39 UTTKh were completed in 1992, the Soviet Union had been dissolved and replaced by a commonwealth of Independent states, the customer now being the Russian Federation, which had inherited the Soviet Union's submarine based element of the nuclear deterrent. To pave the way for flight testing of the complex a series of tests were conducted from a ground-based test stand whereby, as stated in Makeyev documentation, 'flight development tests of missiles dropped from a floating stand', were conducted, there being seven such launches. Further development testing included tests of, as detailed in Makeyev documentation, 'a separation system of the missile shock absorption system with full-scale mockups', four such launches being conducted. Further testing included what Makeyev termed 'tryout stage separation processes'. There were nineteen launches of the K65M-R LV (launch vehicle) in order to prove the carriage and flight characteristics of the middle-yield warheads.

Joint state flight tests commenced with a launch in November 1993. This launch, along with the remaining two - one in December 1994 and the other in November 1997 - being considered failures. In September 1998, as the technicalities of the program were being worked on, the Russian Federation government announced the cancellation of the D-19UTTKh complex with the R-39UTTKh. This decision was taken in response to a proposal recommending same by the Ministries of Economy and Defence. Almost a year prior it had been determined that the D-19UTTKh/R-39UTTKh complex was 73% ready for service and the modifications to the Project 941U submarine missile carrier was considered to be 83.7% complete.

In 2017, one Project 941U, armed with R-39U missiles, remained in operational service (with a trials role added) with the Russian Federation Northern Fleet whilst several boats of the class remained in storage at Severodvinsk. PA Sevmash

Page 111-114 top: The Project 941U Heavy Ballistic Missile Cruiser *Dmitry Donskoy* at the Russian Naval Review at St Petersburg in 2017. Above: The *Dmitry Donskoy* leading an auxiliary replenishment vessel followed by a surface combatant. Above: The fourth generation Russian SLBM's would be designed for carriage in modified Project 667BDR and Project 677BDRM boats. MODRF/PA Sevmash

Although sharing a common numerical index designation with the R-29R, the R-29RM was, to all intents and purposes, a new generation ballistic missile compared with its forebear. The RM added a new third stage, resulting in a length increase of 0.2 m over that of the R-29R, the first and second stages being of slightly differing diameter to the R-29R first and second stages. Makeyev

The three-stage R-29RM (D-9RM complex), development of which commenced in 1979 under general designer V. P. Makeyev with Yu. A. Kaverin appointed leading designer, entered operational service with the Soviet Navy in 1986 (10 MIRV capability) and 1987 (4 MIRV capability). The D-9RM complex was allocated the technological index serial 3M-37, the Soviet rocket index PCM-54 and the NATO reporting designation SS-N-23. To carry and launch the R-29RM a new generation SSBN was designed by CDB-Rubin - the Project 667BDRM Strategic Missile Carrier (allocated the NATO reporting name 'Delta' IV). The first of seven Project 667BDRM submarines (all built by PA Sevmash), which was developed from the Project 667BDR, was completed at Severodvinsk in 1984.

The three-stage R-29RM missile was designed within the constraints present in the limited area of the missile silos that could be made available on the Project 667BDRM. The first stage contained the stage engine and stage fuel tanks, the second stage contained the stage engine and stage fuel tanks and the third stage contained the stage engine, fuel tank, warhead section and instrumentation section. The first stage engine actually consisted of a duel propulsion unit, a single chamber main engine and a four chamber steering engine. Control in pitch/yaw and roll would be provided by, as laid down in Makeyev documentation 'turning the combustion chambers of the steering unit'.

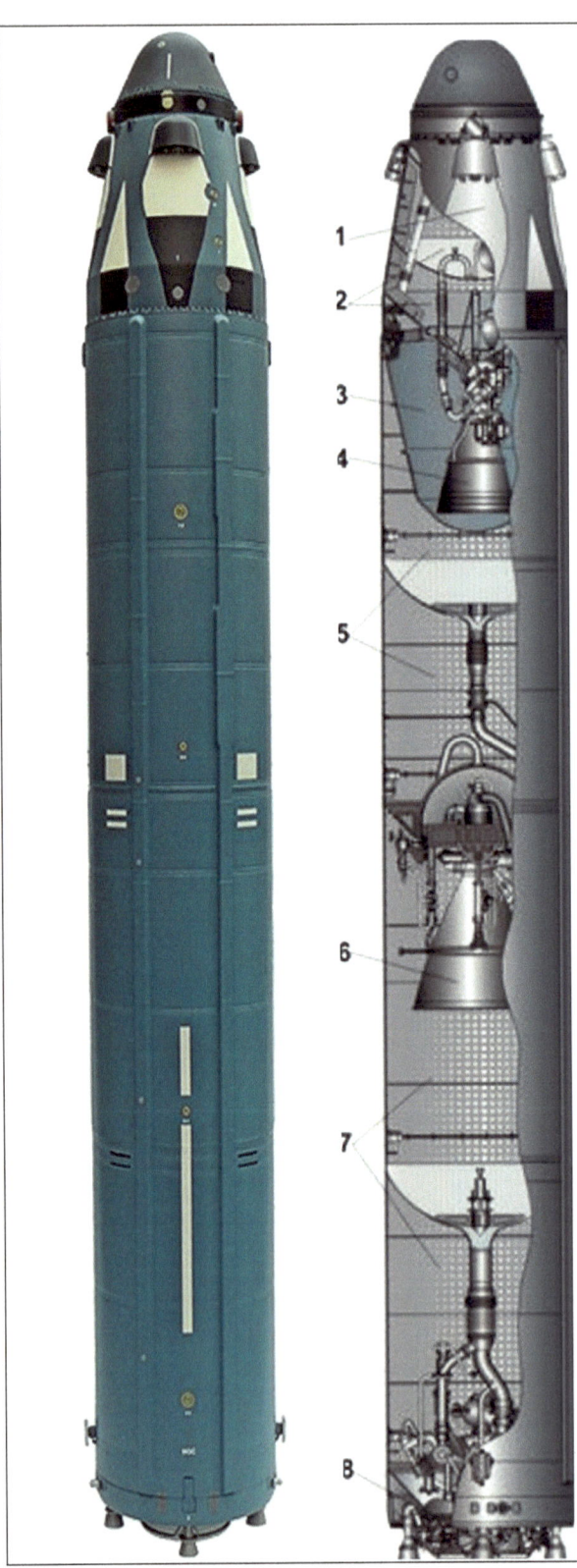

Graphics showing two views of the R-29RM from different elevations. The port side graphic shows the external lines of the R-29RM while the starboard side graphic shows a ghosted view of the R-29RM with the internal compartments numbered:

1. MIRVed warheads
2. 3rd stage and MIRVed warhead fuel tanks
3. Warhead section
4. 3rd stage engine
5. 2nd stage fuel tanks
6. 2nd stage engine
7. 1st stage fuel tanks
8. 1st stage engine

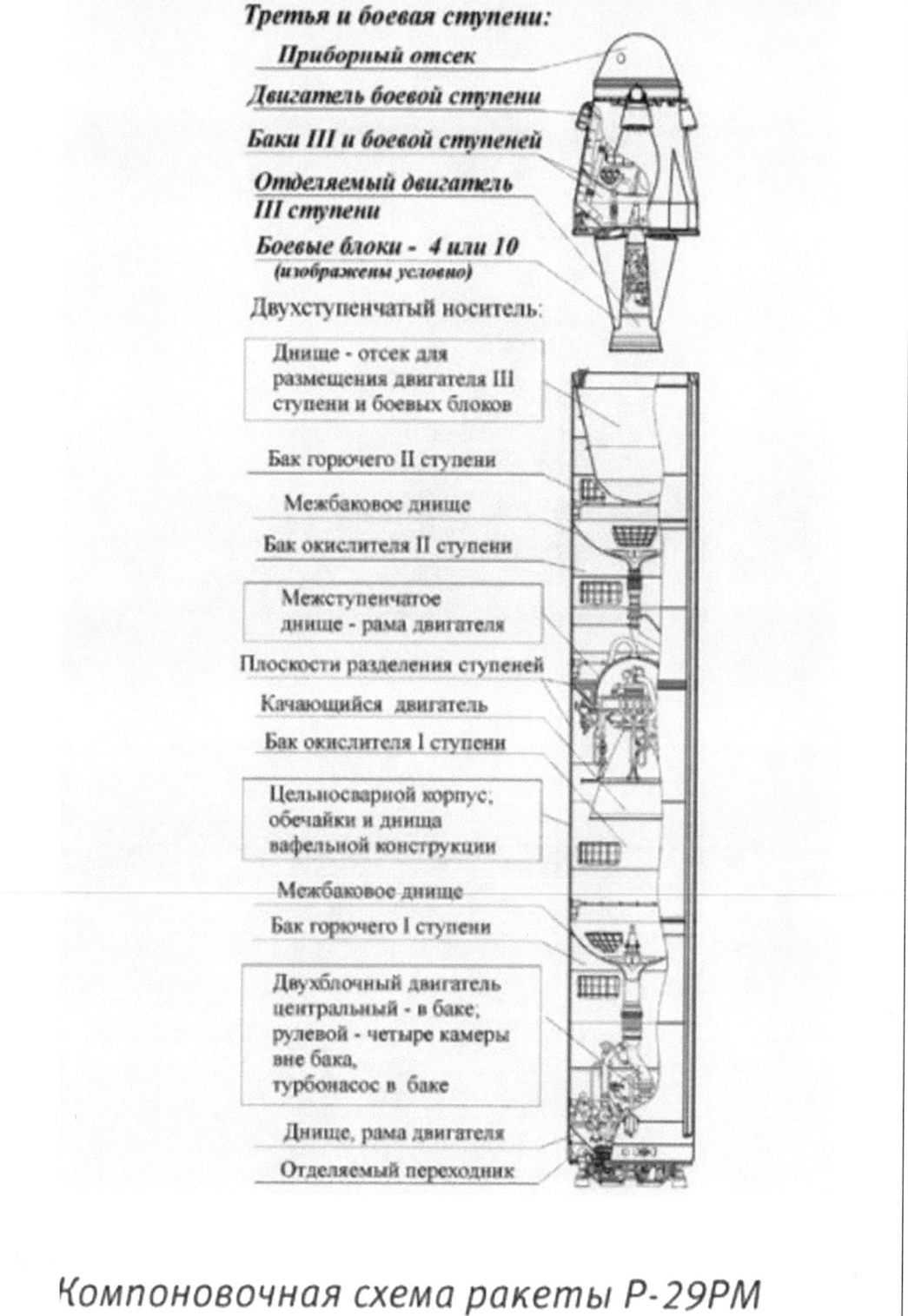

Компоновочная схема ракеты Р-29РМ

Previous page: Non-standard dialect Russian language graphic of the R-29RM(PM) that depicts various areas of significance, including the three stage sections, stage engines, stage propulsion tanks, MIRVed warhead section and the instrumentation section. Above: R-29RM first stage engine. Makeyev

Third stage of the R-29RM ballistic missile with the third stage engine nozzle protruding. Makeyev

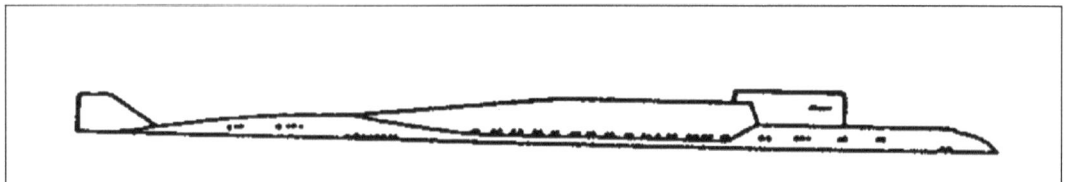

Top: Basic layout diagram of the Project 667BDRM ballistic missile submarine taken from a late 1980's US intelligence document. Above: In the late 1980's Project 667BDRM's began to be increasing encountered by NATO maritime assets. US DoD

The structure of the second stage contained an oxidizer tank that was itself attached to the first stage structure. The second stage also incorporated a fuel tank with a conoidal shape bottom, facilitating accommodation of the protrusion of the third stage engine. The major components of the second stage single-chamber engine were placed within the first stage oxidizer tank. The engine could provide pitch and yaw control via a gimballed combustion chamber, roll control being facilitated by a roll control unit. The incorporation of a third stage added a mere 0.2 m to the overall length of the R-29RM over that of the two-stage R-29. The single chamber third stage engine provided control in all channels, this operating in concert with the duel-mode dispensing engine for the reentry vehicles carrying the warhead(s).

Seven Project 667BDRM strategic missile carrying submarines were built by PA Sevmash at Severodvinsk. The first of these was completed by 1984 and attained an operational capability with the Soviet Navy in 1986 armed with R-29RM. The Project 667BDRM was the cornerstone of the Russian Federation Northern Fleet strategic missile submarine force through the 1990's and into the 21st century. The Project 667BDRM, under 2017 planning, is expected to remain in service until at least 2024 and possibly out to around 2030. US DoD/CDB-Rubin

Project 667BDRM strategic missile carrier submarine. MODRF

In describing the R-29RM Makeyev documentation states 'The two-stage liquid-fuel sustainers are "submerged" in the missile fuel tanks. The design feature of the missile is integration of the 3rd stage propulsion systems and the warhead into a single unit with common tanks. The front section of the missile houses an instrument section with the missile control system, which includes: equipment for astro-correction of the flight trajectory according to the results of measurement of navigation star coordinates, devices for radio correction according to the results of exchanging information with navigational satellites and reentry vehicles'.

Two types of warhead were developed for the R-29RM, a high-speed low yield class, ten of which could be accommodated, and a middle yield warhead, four of which could be accommodated. The reentry vehicles would be dispensed, as stated in Makeyev documentation, 'within an arbitrary zone'. As well as the increased combat potential of the new MIRV's, accuracy of the system was increased through the astro-inertial control system employing satellite navigation radio correction courtesy of the GLONASS (Globanaya Navigozionnaya Sputnikovaya Sistema - Global Positioning System), the complex also retaining the celestial correction navigation system of its forebear.

As with previous generation missiles, the Soviet Union, with the D-9RM complex, continued to improve the capabilities for operating and lunching at high Arctic latitudes in line with Soviet defence doctrine, which advocated the use of the Arctic region for strategic attack against the continental United States. The D-9RM complex was also designed to fly under several flight trajectories against strategic targets, even at close and intermediate ranges, this capability being further developed with the R-29RMU.

An R-29RM ballistic missile is hoisted to or from a shore based test silo. Makeyev

Top: An R-29RM on a transport trolley during factory testing. Above: The Warhead and instrumentations stage of the R-29RMU ballistic missile. Makeyev

The R-29RM/RMU/Project 667BDRM (top) combination, together with the R-29R/RL/RK/Project 667BDR and the R-39/U/Project 941/U missile and missile carrying submarines formed the major nuclear strike force of the Russian Federation Navy in the first two decades after the dissolution of the Soviet Union on 25 December 1991, serving the Northern Fleet (above) and the Pacific Fleet. Makeyev

The three-stage R-29RMU, development of which commenced in 1986 under general designer I. I. Velichko with Yu. A. Kaverin appointed leading designer, entered operational service in 1988. This variant emerged as an update of the R-29RM, the main intention of which was to increase the resistance of the missile complex to the effects of a nuclear explosion. The R-29RMU also expanded on the capability to be successfully launched, with high confidence, from 'high Arctic latitudes', allowing it to be fired along so called 'flat trajectories' with very short flight time to its target in the continental United States, vastly reducing detection times and thus, the time available for potential missile defences to be employed. The payload section contained four MIRV's with medium yield warheads and the possibility to replace these with a ten MIRV low-yield warhead payload. Modifications to the submarine weapon control system allowed the R-29RMU to be put in operation alongside unmodified R-29RM missiles aboard the Project 667BDRM submarines of the Russian Federation Northern Fleet.

R-29RM/RMU1/RMU2 (D-9RM complex) – data furnished by OJSC Makeyev State Rocket Centre

Launch mass: 40.3 tons
Maximum throw weight: 2.8 tons (2800 kg)
Length: 14.8 m
Diameter of first and second stages: 1.9 m
Diameter of third stage: 1.85 m
Number of stages: 3
Fuel: liquid
Control system: astro-radio-inertial
Type of reentry vehicle: 4 warhead MIRVed
Firing range: intercontinental
Force of sea for missile launch: all-weather
Carrier vessel: Project 667BDRM
Number of missiles carried by submarine: 16

The R-29RK/RM series formed the basis of the Russian Federations initial move to fourth generation SLBM's in the shape the R-29RKU-02 and R-29RMU1/2/2.1 missile complexes. Makeyev

5

FOURTH GENERATION RUSSIAN SUBMARINE LAUNCHED BALLISTIC MISSILES

With increasing energy of pace following the turn of the century, the Russian Federation, having weathered the worst of the post-Soviet economic hardship that befell that nation in the years immediately following the dissolution of the Soviet Union on 25 December 1991, embarked upon a concerted effort to modernise her armed forces, commencing with the nuclear deterrent. Significant effort was allocated to the development of a new generation of submarine launched ballistic missiles and a new generation of submarine based strategic missile carriers that would emerge as the RSM-56 Bulava (designed by the Moscow Institute of Thermal Technology and apparently allocated the technological index serial 3M-30) SLBM (Submarine Launched Ballistic Missile) and the Project 955/A Borey/A strategic missile carrying submarines. However, to speed modernisation a number of capability enhancements and service life extension programs were conducted on the R-29R/RL/RK/Project 667BDR and the R-29RM/RMU/Project 667BDRM combinations to keep those systems viable into the second half of the 2010's (R-29R/RL/RK/Project 667BDR) and at the least through the first half of the 2020's (R-29RM/RMU/Project 667BDRM) respectively. Among the major areas to be addressed in some of these systems was the ability to defeat projected United States anti-missile defence systems, development of which had gathered pace in the late 1990s and further accelerated in the first decade of the twenty first century.

The first of these modernisation programs concerned production of a modified design of the R-29RMU missile designated R-29RMU1 Stantcia (Station) of the (D-9RMU1 complex. The design phase of this program commenced in 1996 under general designer V. G. Degtair, chief designer Yu. A. Kaverin and leading designer B. A. Smirnov. The major capability enhancements were in the areas of improved accuracy and survivability against nuclear blasts. The state flight test phase of the program was completed in July 2001, this covering three missile launches in several telemetric configurations, paving the way for the service entry of the complex aboard a Project 667BDRM Strategic Missile Carrier in 2002.

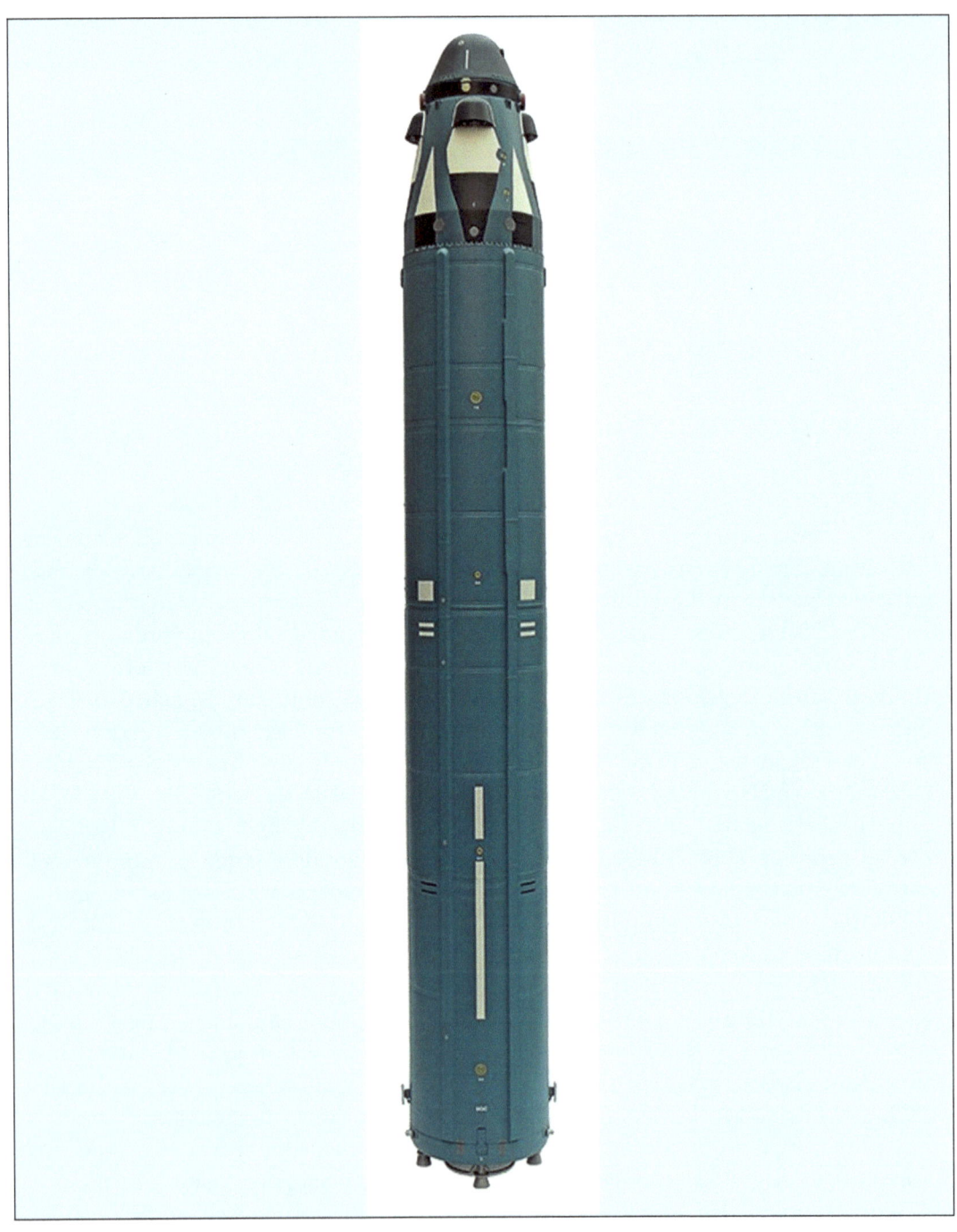

The **R-29RMU1 Stantcia (Station)** of the D-9RMU1 complex was the first major step in the post-Soviet era modernisation of the Russian Federations submarine launched ballistic missile element of the nuclear deterrent triad. Makeyev

Previous page: Russian language graphic showing the various compartments of the R-29RMU1. Text reproduced below with English translation non-bolded in parenthesis: **треья и боевая ступени:** (tray and combat stage:) **приборный отсек и отсек гиропборов** (instrument compartment and compartment gyro); **двигатель боевой ступени** (thruster engine); **баюи третьей и боевой ступеней** (third and combat stages); **отделяемый двигатель третьей ступени** (detachable third stage engine); **4 бовые бпоки** (4 fighting blocks [warheads]); **(показаны условно) двуступенчатый носитель** (shown conditionally two stage carrier); **переднее днище - отсек для размещения третьей ступеи и боевых бпоков** (front bottom compartment for the third stage and combat stage [warhead compartment]); **бак горючего второй ступни** (second stage fuel tank); **двухспойное межбаковое анище** (two lane inter-brake …); **бак окислителя второй стпени** (second stage oxidant tank); **однослойное межступенчатое днище - рама двигателя** (single layer inter-stage floor – engine frame); **4 линхи раздепения ступеней** (4 lynch stages); **качающийся двигатель второй ступени, замюнутая** (rocking second stage engine, muffled); **бак окислителя первой ступени** (oxidizer tank of the first stage); **цельносварной корпус носителя; обечайки и днища вафельной конструкции** (all welded body of the carrier; shells and bottoms of wafer construction); **двухслойное межбаковое днище** (double ply interbake bottom); **двухблочный двигатель первой** (two unit engine of the first stage); **ступени: чентральный-замкнутый, в баке горючегоь; рулевой - замкнутый, четырехкамерный, камеры вне бака, тна в бака** (steps: central-closed, in a tank of fuel; helmsman – closed, four chamber, chamber outside the tank, ton in the tank); **коническое днище, рама двигателя** (conical bottom engine frame); **переходник (в полете не участвует)** (adaptor - does not participate in flight). **This page: The implementation of modernised missiles of the R-29RMU and R-29RKU series was implemented as Project 667BDRM and Project 667BDR submarines entered modernisation and overhaul.** Makeyev/Onega

The R-29RKU2 Stantcia-2 (Station-2) of the D-9RKU2 complex was the only significant early twenty first century modernisation implemented for the missile armament of the Project 667BDR Strategic Missile Carriers of the North Eastern Grouping (Pacific Fleet). Makeyev

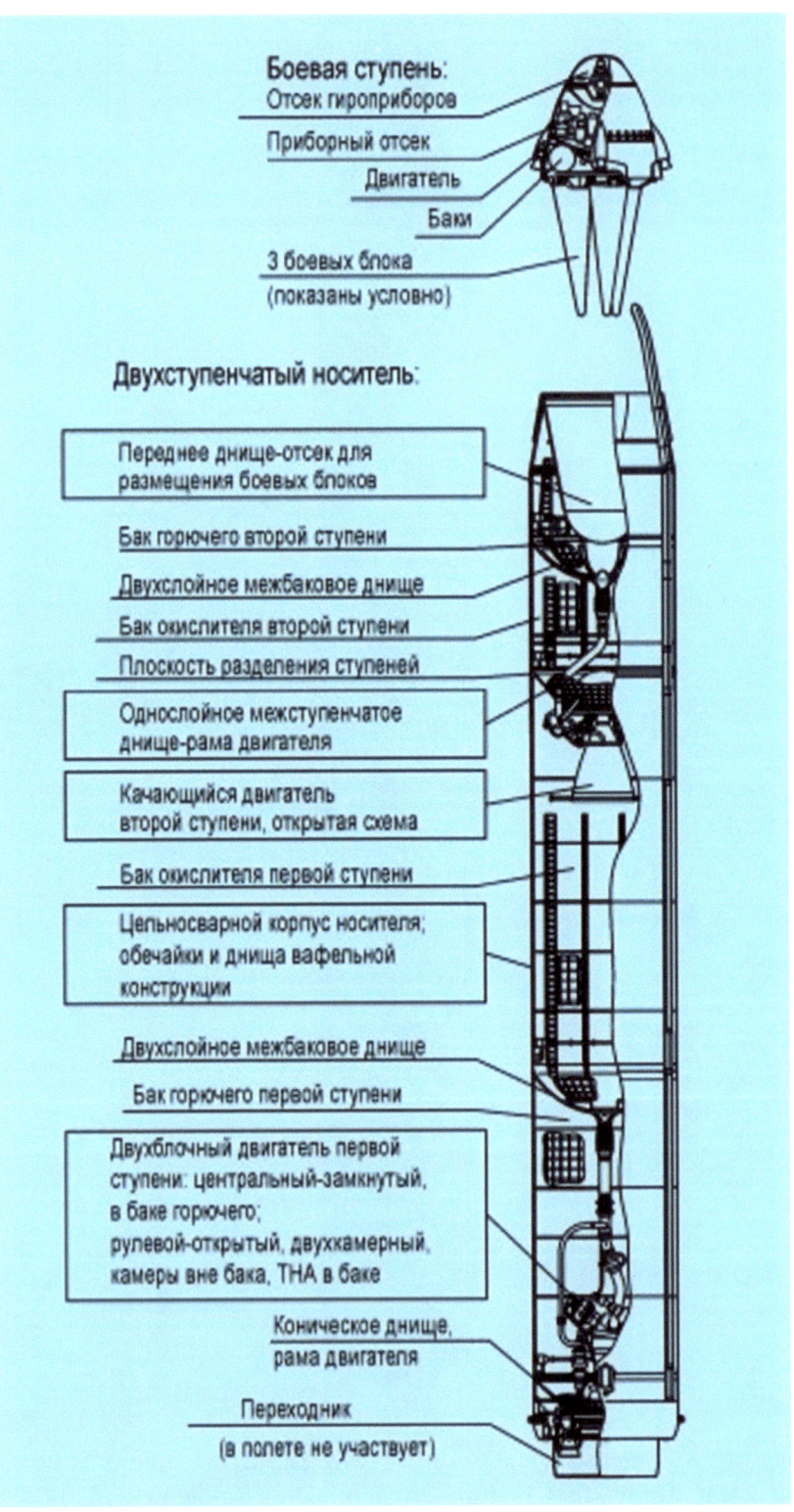

Previous page: Russian language graphic showing the various compartments of the R-29RKU1 missile. Text reproduced below with English translation non-bolded in parenthesis): **боевая ступеньЬ: отсек гиролрибсрсе** (combat stage: gyro compartment); **Двигатепь** (motor); **Баки** (pots); **з боевых бпока (показаны условно)** (from combat vehicle (block), shown conditionally); **двуступенчатый носителв:** (two-stage carrier); **переднее днище-отсек для размещения боавых бпоко** (front bottom compartment for placing booby booms [decoys – penetration aids]); **бак горючего второй ступени** (second stage fuel tank); **двухслоиное межбаковое днище** (double layer inter-brake bottom); **бак озиспитепя второй ступени** (second stage tank, oxygen); **плоскость разделения ступеней** (plane separation of stages); **однослокное межступенчатое днище-рама двигателя** (single layer inter-stage engine bottom frame); **качающийся двигатель второй ступени, открытая схема** (rocking engine of the second stage open circuit); **бак окиспитепя првой ступени** (first stage oxidizer tank); **цепьносварной корпус носителя, обечайки и днища еафепьной; конструкции** (chain of the welded case of the carrier, shell and bottom of the epinephelus construction); **двухслойное межбаковое днище** (doubly layer inter-brake bottom); **бак горючего первой ступени** (first stage fuel tank); **авухблочный авигатеп первой ступнй; чентральный-заикнутый в баке гореочего: рулевой-открытый, двухкамерный, камеры вне бака, тна в баке** (steering open, two chamber, chamber outside the tank… in the tank); **коническое днище, рама двигателя** (conical bottom, engine frame); **переходник (в полете не участвует)** (adaptor - does not participate in flight). This page: A number of yards conducted Project 667BDR/BDRM overhaul and modernisation work, including Zvezdochka Shipyard in Severodvinsk. Makeyev/Bius

While the R-29RMU1 program had been implemented for carriage on the Project 667BDRM Strategic Missile Carriers the R-29RKU-02 Stantsia-2 (Station-2), design development of which commenced in 2003 under general designer V. G. Degtair, chief designer Yu. A. Kaverin and leading designer B. A. Smirnov, was intended for carriage on the Project 667BDR Strategic Missile Carriers. This missile/submarine combination entered service with what had become the Russian Federation Navy North Eastern Group (Pacific Fleet) in 2006. In effect, the R-29RKU-02 was developed as a service life extension program for the R-29RKU-01 missile carried on the Project 667BDR Strategic Missile Carriers of the North Eastern Group, with a service life extending out to 2017 (this may be extended further for a few boats).

In July 1998, the Russian Federation government authorised a modernisation program for the Project 667BDRM Strategic Missile Carrier fleet. This included groundwork into meeting the requirement for future production or modernisation of R-29RMU (D-9RMU complex) ballistic missiles. In October 1998, authorisation was granted for a modernisation of the D-9RMU complex (incorporating the R-29RMU) leading to the D-9RMU2 (incorporating the R-29RMU2 Sineva), which was developed under general designer V. G. Degtair, chief designer Yu. A. Kaverin and leading designer B. A. Smirnov. As the Sineva program progressed through the design stage, a January 2000 decision was taken to implement the program within the existing dimensions of the R-29RMU missile and retain the four warhead MIRV capability with the option to, if required, increase this to a ten MIRV capability. An engineering mock-up of the R-29RMU2 was produced allowing ground development work to progress, paving the way for state flight tests, which commenced in 2003 and were successfully concluded in June 2004.

The resultant D-9RMU2 complex, deployed in 2007, incorporated, as stated in Makeyev documentation 'a R-29RMU2 missile equipped with medium-class combat units [medium yield warheads] developed in the Stantsia experimental design anti-missile defence facilities'. This indicated that the R-29RMU2 design was armed with a new, or at least modified, warhead design that incorporated undisclosed measures to counter NATO (primarily United States) efforts to produce a missile defence system during the first decade of the twenty first century. A new Russian designed onboard control system was incorporated and some elements of the fire control systems of third generation missiles of the R-29RMU and the cancelled R-39UTTKh (UTTH) update of the R-39U, were incorporated, accuracy apparently being improved over that of its forebears. Other elements of the D-9RMU2 complex included what Makeyev described as a 'system of "small" telemetry' and modernisation of the ground based test and maintenance equipment.

The modernisation of the Project 667BDRM Strategic Missile Carriers included incorporation of the Arbat-U2 shipborne digital computer system. This system was designed to allow any combination of R-29RM series missiles to be carried on and launched from the Project 667BDRM submarine. To facilitate the operation of the R-29RMU2.1, Project 667BDRM submarines were fitted with the enhanced capability Arbat-U2.1 computer system.

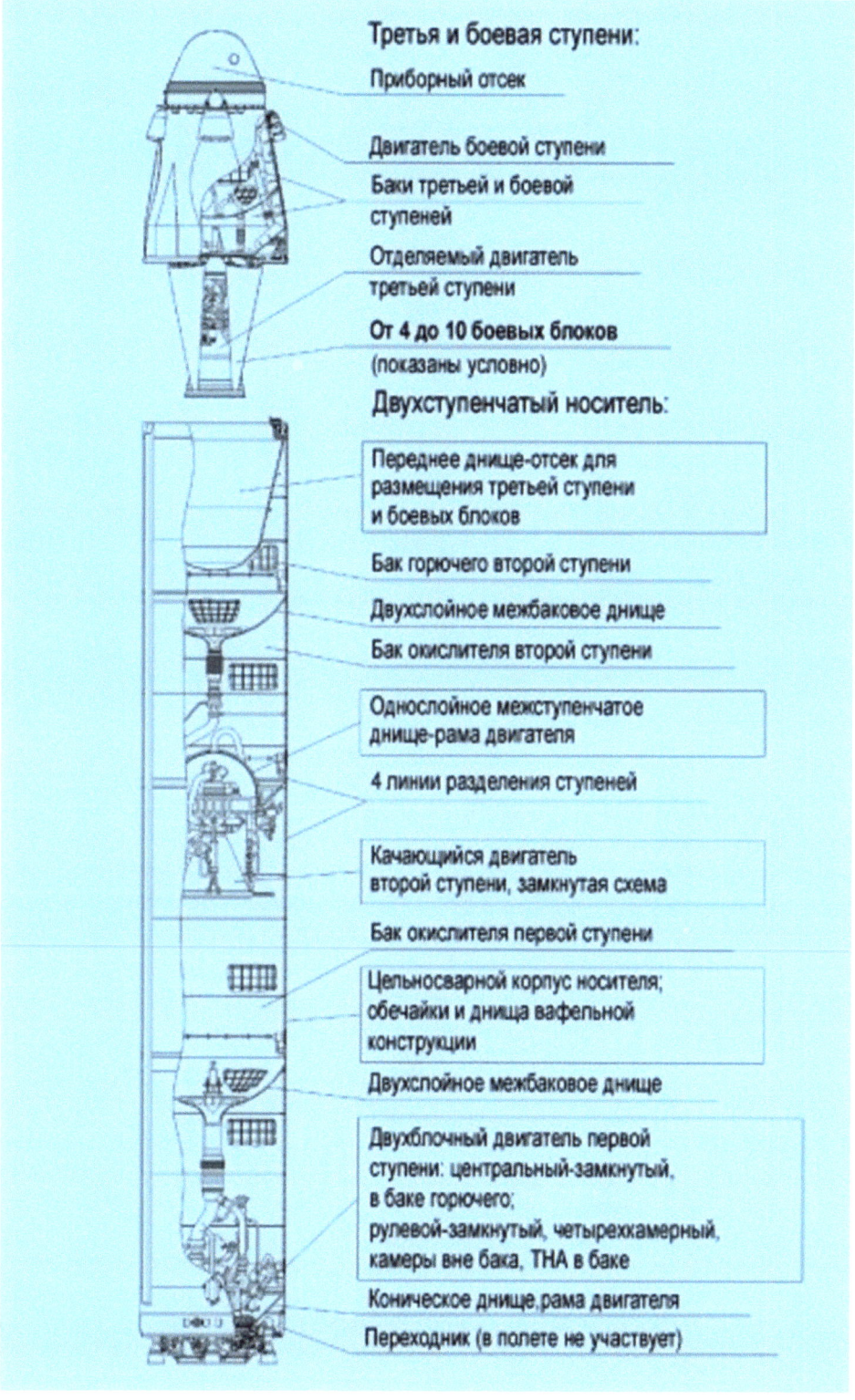

Previous page: Russian language graphic showing the various compartments of the R-29RMU2 missile. Text reproduced below with English translation non-bolded in parenthesis): третья и боевая ступени: (third and combat stages:) **приборный отсек** (instrument compartment); **двигатель боевой стуиени** (combat stage engine); **баки третьей и боевой ступеней** (tanks of the third and combat stages); **отделяемый двигатель третьей ступени** (detachable third stage engine); **от 4 до 10 боевых блоков (показаны условно)** (from 4 to 10 combat units [MIRVed warheads] - shown conditionally); **двухступенчатый носитель:** (two-stage carrier:); **переднее днище-отсек для размещения третьей ступени и боевых блоков** (front bottom compartment for placing the third stage and combat units); **бак горючего второй ступени** (second stage fuel tank); **двоеухслойное межбаковое днище** (two-layered inter-basket bottom); **бак окислителя второй ступени** (second stage oxidizer tank); **однослойное межступенчатое днище-рама двигателя** (single-layer inter-stage engine bottom frame); **4 линии разделения ступеней** (4 lines of separation of steps); **качающийся двигатеь второй ступени, замкнутая схема** (rocking second stage engine, closed circuit); **бак окисгителя первом ступени** (first stage oxidizer tank); **цельносварной корпус носителя; обечайки и днища вафепьной конструюции** (all welded body of the carrier; shells and bottoms of wafer construction); **двухспойное межбаковое днище** (double spaced interbake bottom); **двухблочный двигатеь первой дтупени:** (two unit [chamber] motor of the first stage:); **чентральный-замкнутый, в баке горючего;** (central closed in the fuel tank;); **рулевой-замкнутый, четырехкамерный, каиеры вне бака, тма в баке** (steering closed, four chamber, outside the tank, in the tank); **кснические днище, рама двигателя** (axle head engine frame); **переходник (в полете не участвут)** (adaptor - does not participate in flight).
This page: A Project 667BDRM armed with R-29RMU2 missiles. Makeyev

An R-29RMU2 missile being loaded onto a Project 667BDRM Strategic Missile Carrier. Makeyev

Top: An R-29RMU2.1 ballistic missile is loaded into a dock based test silo. Above: A Project 667BDR armed with R-29RKU2 ballistic missiles. Makeyev/MODRF

Previous page: The Project 677BDR Strategic Missile Carrier *St George the Victorious* of the North Eastern Group (Pacific Fleet) maneuvering and docked in harbor in extreme ice conditions. This page top: The *St George the Victorious*, in relatively benign sea conditions, is maneuvered by a tug to its mooring. Above: The *St George the Victorious* docked alongside a sister ship Project 677BDR. MODRF

Top: A Project 677BDR of the Russian Federation Navy North Eastern Group (Pacific Fleet) in broken ice covered coastal waters off the Russian Federation Far East. Above: A Pacific Fleet Project 667BDR in more open water with the Russian Federation Far East coast in the background. MODRF

Page 142-144: The Project 667BDRM submarine *Tula* in the Zvezdochka Shipyard, Severodvinsk, Arkhangelsk region of Russia, and at roll out following modernisation/refit. Top: A Project 667BDRM submarine is rolled out post refit. Centre and above: The Project 667BDRM Strategic Missile Carrier *Tula* departs from the Zvezdochka Shipyard following completion of post modernization/refit shipyard trials on 21 December 2017. Star

Under 2017 planning the Project 677BDR/R-29RKU series combination was on the verge of retirement and the Project 677BDRM/R-29RMU2/2.1 combination was scheduled to serve until at least 2024. Makeyev

Among the new capabilities introduced in the R-29RMU2, which, as laid down in Makeyev documentation, is a missile with 'the highest energy perfection among domestic [Russian] and foreign naval and land based strategic missiles', including, as further laid down in Makeyev documentation, 'increased sizes of circular and arbitrary zones for the development of combat blocks [deployment of MIRVed warheads]'. The missile can also, as laid down in Makeyev documentation, be flown in 'application of flat trajectories' throughout the entire engagement range, short, medium or long (intercontinental) employing astro-inertial or GPS (Global Positioning System) navigation, the latter through receipt of data inputs from the GLONASS (Globanaya Navigozionnaya Sputnikovaya Sistema) satellite constellation. The range capabilities of the R-29RMU2 were aptly demonstrated in an operational service test launch of the system in 2008. During this test, conducted over the Pacific Ocean, the missile flew a distance of 11500 km.

A further development of the R-29RMU2 Sineva series resulted in the R-29RMU2.1 Lainer (Liner), development of which commenced in 2009 under general designer V. G. Degtair, chief designer Yu. A. Kaverin and leading designer B. A. Smirnov. This missile complex, which entered operational service in 2014, was developed as a countermove to NATO attempts to field an anti-missile defence system. The R-29RMU2.1 was designed to accommodate ten so called small-capacity warhead MRIV's, each featuring enhanced capabilities to defeat NATO anti-missile developments. An alternative loading was eight warheads of the same type as the ten warhead load out, but with a further enhancement of the countermeasures suite, probably in the form of increased advanced decoy dispensing. The third warhead option was four MIRVed medium class with yet further capabilities against anti-missile defence systems. The design of the warhead section allowed for the carriage of a mix of warhead types.

The Project 955 Strategic Missile Carrier, armed with sixteen RSM-56 Bulava ballistic missiles, will, along with the enhanced capability Project 955A, become a stalwart of the Russian Federation submarine based element of that nation's nuclear deterrent triad into the 2040's and possibly beyond. Makeyev

As noted above, CDB-Rubin designed a new generation ballistic missile carrying submarine to carry a new generation ballistic RSM-53 Bulava missile for service from the second decade of the twenty first century. This emerged as the Project 955 Borey Strategic Missile Carrier, which was to supersede the Project 667BDR Strategic Missile Carriers of the Pacific Fleet and the Project 667BDRM Strategic Missile Carriers of the Northern Fleet. The Project 955, which was developed by CDB-Rubin under the design leadership of general designer S. N. Kovalev, with chief designer V. A. Zdornoc (chief designer from 2007 was S. O. Sukhanov), was, as stated in CDB-Rubin documentation, central to the design of the 'basic decision making' for the future direction of Russian missile carrying submarine development.

The Project 955 submarines were built by PA Sevmash at Severodvinsk. The first such vessel, the *Yuri Dolgorukiy*, received a certificate of acceptance on 29 December 2012, paving the way for the vessel to be commissioned in a flag raising ceremony on 13 January 2013. Following a series of service trials this vessel joined the Russian Federation Northern Fleet in October 2015. A further two Project 955 class submarines, the *Alexander Nevsky* and the *Vladimir Monomakh*, were built at Severodvinsk, the latter vessel conducting sea trials in early July 2014 before being commissioned into the Russian Federation Navy on 26 December that year. These three submarines, under 2017 planning, would be followed by no less than five vessels of the Borey-A class to be built at Severodvinsk. The *Knyaz (Prince) Vladimir*, laid down on 21 July 2012, and the *Knyaz (Prince) Oleg*, laid down at on 27 July 2014 to be followed by the *Generalissimo Suvorov*, the *Emperor Alexander III* and the *Knyaz (Prince) Pozharsky*.

In 2017, there had been no official confirmation to speculative reports that the Borey-A submarines were armed with an improved variant of the RSM-56 Bulava and these vessels may well be armed with the same missiles as the Project 955. However, the Ministry of Defence of the Russian Federation has confirmed that the planned Borey-B class will be armed with an improved derivative of the Bulava ballistic missile. Few details of this advancement of the Borey-A have been confirmed other than that improvements to the weapon system will be introduced. Numbers to be built have not been confirmed, but no less than two Borey-B would be required to complete replacement of the seven Project 667BDRM and the 3-4 Project 667BDRM boats that were operational in the second half of the 2010's.

Test launches of the Bulava complex were conducted from the White Sea region off North West Russia with the flights taking place over the Arctic Ocean and North Russia to impact the Russian Kura test range on the Kamchatka Peninsula in the Russian Far East. The first of these test launch was conducted on 23 September 2004. A further 20 test launches were conducted up to 10 September 2010, fourteen of the twenty one launches being assessed as successful with the remaining seven being classified as unsuccessful. However, by that time the major problems dogging the program had been solved with four successful launches between 29 October 2010 and 24 September 2014. Several more launches were conducted over the next year or so, clearing the complex for an initial operational capability with the Russian Northern Fleet in 2015.

RSM-56 Bulava – data furnished by TASS

Maximum range: intercontinental (~8000 km)
Start weight: 36.8 tons
Throw weight: 1150 kg
Length: 12.1 m
Diameter: 2 m
Stages: 3
Warheads: 6-10

Previous page: Successful launch of an RSM-56 Bulava ballistic missile from the submerged Project 955 submarine *Yury Dogoruky* of the Russian Federation Northern Fleet. Top: The first of the Project 955 Strategic Missile Carriers was the *Yury Dogoruky*. Above: The second Project 955 Strategic Missile Carrier, *Alexander Nevsk*y, docked at the Russian naval base in the frozen Krasheninnikov Bay on the Kamchatka Peninsula in the Russian Far East. PA Sevmash/MODRF

Previous page: Russian submarines of the Northern and Pacific fleets regularly have to operate in waters that are partially frozen over. This page: The third Project 955 submarine, *Vladimir Monomakh*, was laid down in March 2006, launched in December 2012 and commissioned in 2014. MODRF

Page 152-153 top: Project 955 Strategic Missile Carriers of the Russian Federation Pacific Fleet. Above: The second Project 955 submarine, *Alexander Nevsky*, berthed in the frozen sea at Krasheninnikov Bay. MODRF

Unidentified Project 955 submarine, probably from the Northern Fleet (assumption based on the coastal features, but unconfirmed). MODRF

RSM-56 Bulava submarine launched ballistic missiles launched from submerged Project 955 Strategic Missile Carriers. The Top photograph shows a missile launched from the *Vladimir Monomakh*, but the launch shown in the bottom photograph is from an unidentified submarine, which may well be the *Vladimir Monomakh*. MODRF

Project 955/A Borey class Strategic Missile Carriers, each carrying sixteen RSM-56 Bulava intercontinental range ballistic missiles. Each missile can carry up to 10 warheads if the operational situation calls for such a load out. A more typical load-out may well be the six warhead grouping. MODRF

Top and above: Unidentified Project 955 Strategic Missile Carrier's. MODRF

Eight Project 955/A Strategic Missile Carriers have been built or are planned for the Russian Federation Navy – data furnished by CDB-Rubin, PA Sevmash and MODRF

Submarine name	Laid Down	Launched	Commissioned
Yuri Dolgoruky (955)	November 1996	February 2008	January 2013
Alexander Nevsky (955)	March 2004	December 2010	December 2013
Vladimir Monomakh (955)	March 2006	December 2012	2014
Kynaz Vladimir (955A)	21 July 2012	17 November 2017	
Knyaz Oleg (955A)	27 July 2014		
Generalissimo Suvorov (955A)	July 2014		
Emperor Alexander III			
Kynaz Pozharsky			

Top: **A Project 955/A submarine during an emergency surface practice.** Above: **A Project 955/A submarine cruises in Northern Waters.** MODRF

As with its predecessors of the Project 667BDR/BDRM and Project 941U classes, the Project 955/A Borey/A class Strategic Missile Carriers, along with the later Borey-B class, all armed with variants of the RSM-56 Bulava SLBM, will undertake patrols in waters closer to the Russian Federation allowing them to be protected. In addition, in regards to the vessels of the Northern Fleet, the Project 955/A/B may conduct operations under the Arctic ice shelf in times of political tension that have a high risk assessment to potential tip over into war with the NATO alliance. The Borey/A/B class, like its predecessors will also have a pier-side operational role, whereby submarines docked in port can remain on alert to fire their missiles from home port if required.

APPENDICES

Appendix I

Missile	Complex	T/I	C/I	IOC	Submarine Platform
R-11FM	D-1	-	-	1959	AV611
R-13	D-2	4K-50	-	1960	Project 629
R-21	D-4	4K-55	-	1963	Project 658
R-27	D-5	4K-10	PCM-25[1]	1968	Project 667A
R-27U	D-5(U)	4K-10	PCM-25	1974	Project 667A
R-27K	D-5(K)	4K-18	PCM-25	1975	Project 605[2]
R-29	D-9	4K-75	PCM-40	1974	Project 667B
R-29D	D-9D	-	-	1978	Project 667BD
R-29R	D-9R	3M-40	PCM-50	1977	Project 667BDR
R-29RL	D-9RL	3M-40	PCM-50	1979	Project 667BDR
R-29RK	D-9RK	3M-40	PCM-50	1982	Project 667BDR
R-39	D-19	3M-65	PCM-52	1983	Project 941
R-29RM	D-9RM	3M-37	PCM-54	1986	Project 667BDRM
R-29RKU	D-9RK(U)	3M-40	PCM-50	1987	Project 667BDR
R-29RMU	D-9RM(U)	3M-37	PCM-54	1988	Project 667BDRM
R-31	D-11	-	-	1980	Project 667AM
R-39U	D-19(U)	3M-65	PCM-52	1988	Project 941U
R-29RKU-01	D-9RK(U)-01	3M-40	PCM-50	1990	Project 667BDRM
R-39UTTH[3]	D-19UTTH	3M-91	PCM-52 Bap	N/A	Project 941UTTH
R-29RMU1	D-9RM(U)1	3M-37	PCM-52	2002	Project 667BDRM
R-29RKU-02	D-9RK(U)-02	3M-40	PCM-50	2006	Project 667BDR
R-29RMU2	D-9RM(U)2	3M-37	PCM-54	2007	Project 667RBDRM
R-29RMU2.1	D-9RM(U)2.1	3M-37	PCM-54	2014	Project 667BDRM
Bulava	-	3M-30	PCM-56	2015	Project 955

T/I – Technological Index
C/I – Complex Index
IOC – Initial Operational Capability

Note: The submarine platforms listed are the initial platforms on which the respective missile complex attained an operational capability

---

[1] PCM = RSM

[2] The Project 605 was a single conversion from a Project 629 conventional powered ballistic missile submarine

[3] Also referred to as the R-39UTTKh

Appendix II

Russian language graphic detailing the major submarine launched ballistic missile developments by JSC Company 'Academician' V. P. Makeyev State Rocket Centre. English translation is shown in three following groups

Group 1 – First and Second generation SLBM						
Generation	1	1	1	2	2	2
Index of complex	D-1	D-2	D-4	D-5	D-5	D-9
Rocket index	R-11FM	R-13	R-21	R-27	R-27K	R-29
Rocket index contract						
CCCP				PCM-25		PCM-40
USA		SSN-4	SSN-5	SSN-6	SSNX-6	SSN-8
Technological index		4K-50	4K-55	4K-10	4K-18	4K-75
Starting mass, tons	5.47	13.74	19.63	14.3	13.3	33.3
Throw mass, kg	975	1597	1179	650	720	1100
Length, m	10.3	11.8	14.2	9.06	9.0	13.0
Diameter, m	0.88	1.3	1.3	1.5	1.5	1.8
Engine type	ЖРД		ЖРД	ЖРД		ЖРД
Number of stages	1	1	1	1	2	2
Type of control	inertial	inertial	inertial	(inertial + celestial)		
Types of head	(		see main text			)
Maximum range, km	150	600	1420	2500-3000	900	intercontinental
Submarine platform	611/629	629/658	629A/658M	667A(U)	605	667B/BD
Number of missiles	2/3	3/3	3/3	16	4	12/16

Group 2 – Third generation SLBM			
Generation	3	3	3
Index of complex	D-9R	D-19	D-9RM
Rocket index	R-29R	R-39	R-29RM
Rocket index contract			
СССР[4]	РСМ-50	РСМ-52	РСМ-54
USA	SSN-18[5]	SSN-20	SSN-23
Technological index	3М-40	3М-65	3М-37
Starting mass, tons	35.3	84.0	40.3
Throw mass, kg	1650	2250	2800[6]
Length, m	14.6	16.0	14.8
Diameter, m	1.8	2.4	1.9
Engine type	ЖРД[7]	РДТТ[8]	ЖРД
Number of stages	2	3	3
Type of control	АИ[9]	(астроинерциальная (АИР[10]))	
Types of head	(	see main text	)
Maximum firing range	(	intercontinental	)
Submarine platform	667BDR	941	667BDRM
Number of missiles	16	20	16

---

[4] СССР (USSR – Union of Soviet Socialist Republics)

[5] NATO terminology is SS-N

[6] Shown on test to be about 2000 kg when firing at the maximum range

[7] ЖРД (liquid propellant)

[8] РДТТ (solid propellant)

[9] astro-sighting system/astro-correction system

[10] astro-sighting/astro-correction system (enhanced)

Group 3 – Fourth generation SLBM					
Generation	4	4	4	4	4
Index of complex	D-19UTTH[11]	D-9RMU1	D-9RKU-02	D-9RMU2	D-29RMU2.1
Rocket index	R-19UTTH	R-29RMU1	R-29RKU-02	R-29RMU2	R-29RMU2.1
Rocket index contract					
CCCP[12]	PCM-52bap	PCM-54	PCM-50	PCM-54	PCM-54
USA	SSN-20	SSN-23	SSN-18	SSN-23	SSN-23
Technological index	3M-91	-	-	-	-
Starting mass, tons	81.0[13]	40.3	35.3	40.3	40.3
Throw mass, kg	3400(3000)	2800[14]	1650	2800[14]	2800[14]
Length, m	16.1	14.8	14.6	14.8	14.8
Diameter, m	2.4	1.9	1.8	1.9	1.9
Engine type	ратт	жрд	жрд	жрд	жрд
Number of stages	3	3	2	3	3
Type of control	(астроинерциальная (арир[15]))		АИ[16]	(астроинерциальная (арир[17]))	
Head type	MIRV[18]10(8)	MIRV4	MIRV3	MIRV4	MIRV10
Max range	IC[19]	IC	IC	IC	IC
Platform	941U	667BDRM	667BDR	667BDRM	667BDRM
Number of missiles	20	16	16	16	16

Note: The R-39UTTH is described in the chapter text body along with the third generation R-39/U, but technologies developed for this complex conformed to the fourth generation

---

[11] Also referred to as the R-39UTTKh

[12] CCCP (USSR – Union of Soviet Socialist Republics)

[13] Loading weight of the rocket with amortization system is 90 tons (R-39), 86 tons (P-39UTTH)

[14] Shown on test to be about 2000 kg when firing at the maximum range

[15] astro-sighting system/astro-correction system (enhanced)

[16] astro-sighting system/astro-correction system

[17] astro-sighting system/astro-correction system (enhanced)

[18] Multiple Independent Re-entry Vehicle

[19] Intercontinental

Appendix III

Project	Type	Number built	IOC	OOSD	Missiles operated
AV611	SSB	6-7	1959	1980's	R-11FM
629/A	SSB	23[20]	1960	1990	R-11FM/R-13/R-21
658/A	SSBN	8[21]	1960	1991	R-13/R-21
667A/AU	SSBN	34	1968	1995	R-27/U
605	SSB	1[22]	1975	1982	R-27K
667AM	SSBN	1[23]	1980	1990	R-31
667B	SSBN	10	1974	late 1990's	R-29
667BD	SSBN	4	1978	c1996	R-29
667BDR	SSBN	14	1977	N/A[24]	R-27R/RL/RK/RKU/RKU-01/RKU-02
667BDRM	SSBN	7	1986	N/A	R-29RM/RMU/RMU1/2/2.1
941/U	SSBN	7	1983	N/A[25]	R-39/U
955/A	SSBN	8[26]	2015	N/A	RSM-56 Bulava

Note 1: The IOC (Initial Operational Capability) years given reflect just that and not the first commissioning date for the submarine

Note 2: The OOSD (Out Of Service Date) reflects the years for withdrawal as operational SSB/SSBN and does not reflect the other roles that a number of SSB/SSBN were employed in following retirement from the nuclear counterstrike role

Note 3: There were other, non-operational, conversions from submarine projects to test new generation weapons such as the Project 601 conversion from Project 629 B-149 to test the D-9 complex

Note 4: Although stated retirement dates vary between agencies it seems that the last of the Project 629/B submarines were retired from Soviet naval service in 1990. Some were dispatched to North Korea for scrapping, these being the source of unconfirmed reports of such boats in trials with North Korean ballistic missile developments. The last of the Project 658/M submarines was retired in 1991. The last of the Project 667A/U Strategic Missile Carriers was decommissioned in January 1995, bringing to an end the operational role of the R-27/U SLBM. Although various agencies provide conflicting dates, it is clear that the last of the Project 667B Strategic Missile Carriers had been withdrawn from service by 1998. The last of the Project 667BD boats appear to have been retired by 1996

---

[20] Fourteen Project 629 boats were converted to Project 629B standard from 1966 to 1972. One unit was lost when it sank in the Pacific Ocean in 1968

[21] Most of the Project 658 bats were converted to 658M

[22] Single conversion from Project 629

[23] Single cconversion from a Project 667A

[24] The 667BDR was scheduled for retirement in late 2017, but the status of the boats in service in 2017 is unclear in December 2017. At least one or two 667BDR boats are thought to remain in service going into 2018, but may be on the verge of retirement

[25] The *Dmitry Donskoy*, the sole Project 941U submarine remaining in service, has a duel trials/operational role. In the former it was employed as a test platform for new generation missiles, in particular the RSM-56 Bulava and advanced derivatives under development in late 2017. Several other Project 941/U boats remain in storage at Severodvinsk as of late 2017

[26] This is the number announced as of December 2017. Further boats are planned as Project 955B

GLOSSARY

ASCM	Anti-Ship Cruise Missile
ASW	Anti-Submarine Warfare
bhp	Brake Horse Power
CCCP	USSR - Union of Soviet Socialist Republics
CEP	Circular Error Probability
DIA	Defence Intelligence Agency
G-class	Golf class (Project 629 submarine)
GLONASS	Globanaya Navigozionnaya Sputnikovaya Sistema (Global Positioning System satellite constellation)
H-class	Hotel class (Project 658 submarine)
HACC	Heavy Aircraft Carrying Cruiser
ICBM	Inter-Continental Ballistic Missile
II	Roman numeral number 2
IRBM	Intermediate Range Ballistic Missile
JSC	Joint Stock Company
kg	Kilogram
kgf/s/kg	Kilogram Force/per second/per kilogram
km	Kilometer
lb.	Pound (measure of weight)
m	metre
MAD	Mutually Assured Destruction
MIRV	Multiple Independently targetable Reentry Vehicle
MRV	Multiple Reentry Vehicle
MW	Megawatt
NATO	North Atlantic Treaty Organisation
NHHC	Naval History Heritage Centre
NII-1011	Ministry of Medium Machine Building
Nuclear	Atomic energy
OJSC	Open Joint Stock Company
OKB-1	S.P. Korolev Rocket and Space Corporation, Energia
Polynya	Aero of liquid ocean water where sea ice would be expected to form
RORSAT	Radar Ocean Reconnaissance Satellite
SALT	Strategic Arms Limitation Talks
SKB-385	JSC Company 'Academician V.P. Makeyev State Rocket Centre
SLBM	Submarine Launched Ballistic Missile
SMLS	Shock-mounted Missile Launch System
SSB	Conventional powered ballistic missile submarine
SSBN	Nuclear powered ballistic missile submarine
START-1	Strategic Arms Reduction Treaty-1
Thermonuclear	Thermonuclear warhead – utilising the transformation of various nuclei of low atomic weight atoms (for example

	hydrogen - hence the term hydrogen bomb) that would require extremely high temperatures initiate reaction
TNT	Trinitrotoluene – a high explosive chemical formation
Tu	Tupolev
US DoD	United States Department of Defence
USNHC	United States Naval Historical Center
USSR	Union of Soviet Socialist Republics
V/STOL	Vertical/Short Take-Off and Landing
Warsaw Pact	A formal Treaty of Friendship, Co-operation and Mutual Assistance signed between the Socialist Republics of the USSR and 7 Soviet Orbit satellite states in Eastern Europe. This treaty, which took effect from 14 May 1955, was designed to counter the growing NATO alliance opposed to the Eastern Block
°	Degree(s)
±	Plus or minus
~	Approximately equal to (can also be used to mean asymptotically equal)

ABOUT THE AUTHOR

Hugh Harkins, FRAS is a historian and author with an extensive background in astro/geophysics and studies/research in the wider scientific, aeronautic, astronautic and nautical technical and historical fields. Hugh has published in excess of sixty books; non-fiction and fiction, writing under his given name as well as utilising several pseudonyms. He has also written for several international magazines, whilst his work has been used as reference for many other projects ranging from the aviation industry, international news corporations and film media to encyclopaedias, museum exhibits and the computer gaming industry. Hugh is a member of the Institute of Physics and is an elected Fellow of the Royal Astronomical Society. He currently resides in his native Scotland.

Other titles by the author include
Iskander - Mobile Tactical Aero-Ballistic/Cruise Missile Complex
Orbital/Fractional Orbit Bombardment System - The Soviet Globalnaya Raketa
Counter-Space Defence Co-Orbital Satellite Fighter
Sukhoi T-50/PAK FA - Russia's 5th Generation 'Stealth' Fighter
Sukhoi Su-35S 'Flanker' E - Russia's 4++ Generation Super-Manoeuvrability Fighter
Sukhoi Su-34 'Fullback'
Sukhoi Su-30MKK/MK2/M2 - Russo Kitashiy Striker from Amur
MiG-35/D 'Fulcrum' F – Towards the Fifth Generation
Air War over Syria, Tu-160, Tu-95MS & Tu-22M3 - Cruise Missile and Bombing Strikes on Syria, November 2015-February 2016
Sukhoi Su-27SM(3)/SKM
Russian Non-Nuclear Attack Submarines – Project 877/877E/877EKM/Project 636/636.3 & Project 677/Amur 1650/950/S-1000
Russian/Soviet Aircraft Carrier & Carrier Aviation Design & Evolution Volume 1 - Seaplane Carriers, Project 71/72, Graf Zeppelin, Project 1123 ASW Cruiser & Project 1143-1143.4 Heavy Aircraft Carrying Cruiser
Light Battle Cruisers and the Second Battle of Heligoland Bight
British Battlecruisers of World War 1 - Operational Log, July 1914-June 1915
Eurofighter Typhoon - Storm over Europe
Tornado F.2/F.3 Air Defence Variant
Air to Air Missile Directory
North American F-108 Rapier - Mach 3 Interceptor
Convair YB-60 - Fort Worth Overcast
Boeing X-36 Tailless Agility Flight Research Aircraft
X-32 - The Boeing Joint Strike Fighter
X-35 - Progenitor to the F-35 Lightning II
X-45 Uninhabited Combat Air Vehicle
Into The Cauldron - The Lancaster MK.I Daylight Raid on Augsburg
Hurricane IIB Combat Log - 151 Wing RAF, North Russia 1941
RAF Meteor Jet Fighters in World War II, an Operational Log
Typhoon IA/B Combat Log - Operation Jubilee, August 1942
Defiant MK.I Combat Log - Fighter Command, May-September 1940
Blenheim MK.IF Combat Log - Fighter Command Day Fighter Sweeps/Night Interceptions, September 1939 - June 1940
Tomahawk I/II Combat Log - European Theatre, 1941-42

www.ingramcontent.com/pod-product-compliance
Lightning Source LLC
Chambersburg PA
CBHW041542220426
43664CB00003B/33